Irenaeus and

Orthodox Apologetic Methodology:

A Neopatristic Presuppositionalism

Fr. Joshua Schooping

Irenaeus and Orthodox Apologetic Methodology

Preface

Centering itself broadly in the field of systematic theology, and more narrowly in the field of apologetics, the present study argues the case that there is an identifiable and even normative Orthodox apologetic methodology represented in the works of Irenaeus. In order to demonstrate this it begins by relating apologetic motives to methodology, distinguishing method and methodology, and clarifying the argument's basic scope. Following this it contextualizes the study in relation to the complex field of apologetics, especially Reformed Presuppositionalism, and argues that Irenaeus is relevant to this field as an Orthodox articulation of the apologetic task, making possible what be called Neopatristic Presuppositional Apologetics. In order to demonstrate this, this study examines select texts from Irenaeus' extant complete works, specifically the prefaces and conclusions of his *Demonstration of the Apostolic Preaching* together with the five books of his *Adversus Haereses*. Following this, Neopatristic Presuppositionalism provides a critique of Reformed Presuppositionalism, demonstrating that apologetics is on a more secure foundation when undertaken within Orthodoxy.

Irenaeus and Orthodox Apologetic Methodology

CONTENTS

INTRODUCTION	5
STATE OF THE APOLOGETICS QUESTION	8
DEFINING APOLOGETICS	14
IRENAEUS OF LYONS' RELEVANCE TO APOLOGETICS	20
THE IRENAEAN EVIDENCE: AN EXPOSITION IN LIGHT OF APOLOGETICS	23
Demonstration of the Apostolic Preaching	24
Adversus Haereses, or *The Exposure and Refutation of Knowledge Falsely So-Called*	33
Book I	33
Book II	46
Book III	52
Book IV	56
Book V	62
ASSESSMENT IN LIGHT OF CONTEMPORARY	

APOLOGETIC DISCOURSE	68
A NEOPATRISTIC PRESUPPOSITIONAL CRITIQUE OF REFORMED PRESUPPOSITIONALISM	85
PROSPECTUS AND CONCLUSION	94
Appendix 1: A BRIEF EXCURSUS INDICATING ATHANASIUS AND GREGORY OF NYSSA'S CONTINUITY WITH IRENAEUS' APOLOGETIC METHODOLOGY	98
Appendix 2: CONTRA LESSING: A CRITICAL EXAMINATION OF LESSING'S DITCH	103
BIBLIOGRAPHY	139

Irenaeus and Orthodox Apologetic Methodology

INTRODUCTION

The Church Fathers did not practice or approach apologetics whimsically or impressionistically, but with utmost gravity and intentionality. Nor, as though in a vacuum, did they approach it as an abstract exercise of cogitation, nor even as a mere agitated sophistry - which is to say, rhetoric without an intrinsic ethical commitment to particular truth claims. In practicing and approaching apologetics, there was motive. By motive is meant that perceived state of affairs which impels the would-be apologist to undertake apologetical efforts. These states of affairs can be either of a more general nature (as, for example, when dealing with broad concerns such as Gnosticism or Arianism) or a more particular nature (as, for example, when engaged with a specific argument or opponent, e.g. *this* Gnostic argument or *that* Arian opponent). What interests the present study, however, is not primarily the states of affairs in and of themselves, either general or particular, but the manner in which these were translated by the apologist into motive. Moreover, what concerns the present study are those motives which were in some way transmitted in writing.

As will be argued below, a motivation to undertake apologetics was integrated with and informative of methodology. By methodology is meant something more general than any one locally applied method or finite set of particular methods such as, for example, particular argument strategies like *reductio ad absurdum* or *ad hominem*. To utilize, for the purposes of the present discourse, a definition given by Bochenski, "method is the manner of proceeding in any particular field," and, "methodology is the theory of method."[1] Since the field being studied is apologetics, operating as it does within the larger field of systematic theology, apologetic methodology would then be the theory of apologetic method, the theory of how to proceed in the field of apologetics - i.e. the theory underlying the how of "doing apologetics." Consequently, methodological theory is any particular method's presupposition, and method is the application or expression of some methodology.

    Moreover, an apologetic method, instantiating as it does some facet of an apologetic methodology, can be viewed either from a more particular and practical perspective, such as *this* use of *reductio* or *that* charge of self-refutation, or from a more general and theoretical perspective, which in light of the foregoing would be the more general and theoretical observation that there is present a use of logical refutation and charges of logical inconsistency as particular apologetic methods integral within a larger apologetic methodology or framework. When such particular methods are discussed, then, which is inevitable in an analysis of an apologetic text, it will again be from this more general and theoretical perspective, as this relates more directly to the general notion of methodology appropriate to systematic theology. It is thus motive and methodology which are under present inquiry. The present study, operating as it does within a framework of concerns

---

[1] J.M. Bochenski, *The Methods of Contemporary Thought*, (New York, NY: Harper and Row, 1968), 9.

rooted in systematic theology, although looking closely at historic Patristic texts, will thus seek to garner justified insight towards answering questions concerning what "Orthodox" apologetic methodology *is* together with what "Orthodox" motives and methods *are* in a more than merely historiographic sense. In other words, and more directly, looking to Irenaeus of Lyons as emblematic of Orthodox tradition, the present study will seek through him to shed light on what an Orthodox apologetic motivation and methodology is and what that might look like.

It is also worthwhile to note that, in addition to particular arguments, whether or not they are successful arguments or not falls beyond the scope of the present inquiry. Traditional apologetic themes, such as proof of God's existence, the immortality of the soul, or solutions to the problem of evil, are also not of present concern. Likewise, particular theological positions fall beyond the scope of the present inquiry. In other words, whether or not, for example, Irenaeus was arguing for the divinity of Christ, or even whether he was successful in arguing this, is again not precisely the concern when considering specifically Irenaeus' apologetic methodology. Much has been written concerning his theology, but it seems that next to nothing has been directly concerned with "Irenaeus the apologist," much less with either discerning from his work a relevant methodology or asking whether this might speak to the contemporary field of apologetics.[2]

---

[2] Quasten and Behr, to name two of many, both attribute great significance to Irenaeus as a theologian, as will be indicated more below. Though Quasten does recognize the apologetic nature of his work, for some reason Behr does

7

Irenaeus and Orthodox Apologetic Methodology

STATE OF THE APOLOGETICS QUESTION

The question as to what apologetics *is*, as an historical practice, a body of literature, and a present day field, is vast and complex, to say the least, and a summary of its developments and current state is quite beyond the scope of the present study which, to a

---

not seem to treat much, if at all, with Irenaeus' apologetics *as* apologetics. See Johannes Quasten, *Patrology: Vol. 1, The Beginnings of Patristic Literature*, (Westminster, MD: The Newman Press, 1962), 287-313. See also John Behr, *The Way to Nicaea: The Formation of Christian Theology: Vol 1*, (Crestwood, NY: St Vladimir's Seminary Press, 2001), 111-133. See also his book-length treatment of Irenaeus: John Behr, *Irenaeus of Lyons: Identifying Christianity*, (Oxford: Oxford University Press, 2013).

For a persuasive treatment of Irenaeus' *theological* methodology, which in important ways can serve to justify the present further study concerning Irenaeus' apologetical methodology, see: Philip Hefner, "Theological Methodology and St. Irenaeus," The Journal of Religion, Vol. 44, No. 4 (Oct., 1964), pp. 294-309.

It also seems that even the mere inclusion of Irenaeus among the early "apologists" is rare, a situation which is reflected in this typical sentiment: "It is conventional and convenient to treat Aristides, Justin, Tatian, Athenagoras and Theophilus as the main Greek apologetic writers of the second century." See: D. W. Palmer, "Atheism, Apologetic, and Negative Theology in the Greek Apologists of the Second Century," Vigiliae Christianae 37 (1983) 234-259, 237. Dulles doesn't mention Irenaeus among the Greek apologists, and barely at all, in his history on the subject. There is not room to explore the historical reasons for this within the present essay, though one contributing reason seems to be a disparity between the conception of apologetics by historians and Patristic scholars who are not generally interested in apologetics, *per se*, or its relevance to the contemporary field, on the one hand, and apologetics as a living discipline not generally interested in Patristic-era apologetic methodology, on the other. The result is clear, that Irenaeus' potential contribution to apologetics is untapped. Considering the role tradition plays in Orthodoxy, however, the foregoing situation is unsustainable if Orthodoxy is to speak self-consistently to the concerns of apologetics.

large degree, presupposes at least some rudimentary background awareness, if not knowledge.³ That said, since Christians have been defending the faith, via text, since at least the New Testament, containing at the very least apologetic *elements*, it would be unfitting to allow the complex development of the contemporary field of apologetics to obscure this perennial interest of the Church such that its past insights go unmined.⁴ For example, evidence of the Church's longstanding interest in and distinct awareness of apologetics is exemplified in one Arethas, Archbishop of Caesarea in the early Tenth Century, who requested a compilation of a large number of prior apologetic texts "from primitive times down to Eusebius," an enormous work, a *"Corpus Apologetarum"* today compiled into nine Greek-Latin bilingual volumes.⁵ In setting out to accomplish this, at the very least there had to be a rudimentary intuition or notion of a discipline of apologetics, and it also seems that there was to some degree the assumption that these past texts were also to be presently relevant and therefore helpful for accomplishing the then present apologetic needs, despite being at a remove of hundreds of years.

    Some of the obscurity regarding the relationship between apologetics as practiced historically by Church Fathers

---

[3] For perhaps the only book-length historiography of apologetics, see: Avery Cardinal Dulles, *A History of Apologetics*, (San Francisco, CA: Ignatius Press, 2nd ed., 2005).

[4] For the New Testament's being seen as the source of a Christian ground for the practice of apologetics there is abundant literature, one being the aforementioned: Dulles, *A History of Apologetics*, 1-25.

[5] Johannes Quasten, *Patrology: Vol. 1, The Beginnings of Patristic Literature*, (Westminster, MD: The Newman Press, 1962), 188-9.

and as practiced today within the field of apologetics is arguably due to the complex relationship between, on the one hand, the early Church apologists considered merely as subjects of historiography and, on the other hand, the contemporary development of apologetics as a distinct field oriented towards present day applications and concerns, i.e. the close application of apologetics as a discipline to that object with which it is presently engaged. For example, Valentinianism in its historical particularity is presently defunct, and so the apologetics militated against it by Irenaeus are not in any obvious way related, say, to the debates that occur today between Calvinists and Arminians. Thus a Calvinist is not particularly interested, insofar as Calvinism *qua* Calvinism is concerned, with analyzing particular arguments in *Adversus Haereses*, not only because of Calvinism's ambivalent attitude towards Church tradition, but because the prooftexts he might exposit in order to militate against Arminianism is, to all appearances, unrelated to Irenaeus' project. In this sense, early apologetic efforts tend to grow obscure and forgotten.

What this then points to is the further tendency of apologetics to concern itself with contextual arguments that are suited to their particularities to the degree that diachronic methodological concerns are given less, if any, explicit attention. It seems that only in the second half of the Twentieth Century, especially with prior developments by Christian philosophers such as Cornelius Van Til, where the notion of apologetic methodology *qua* methodology is, in and of itself, given sustained attention and distinct development.[6] In other words, it seems that it was during this period where a shift of awareness occurred in regards to apologetics, from that of generating particular arguments (or avoiding apologetics altogether) to one of also discussing explicitly the ways in which apologetics was best to be done.[7] This then has given rise to a

---

[6] See Dulles, 353. For a valuable contribution to the study of certain varieties of apologetic methodology, see: Gordon R. Lewis, *Testing Christianity's Truth Claims: Approaches to Christian Apologetics*, (Chicago: IL: Moody Press, 1976).

Van Til, in the first half of the Twentieth Century, who more than most established the necessity of treating with methodology, is to a large degree following upon the Anti-Modernist issues raised by late Nineteenth, early Twentieth Century Reformed thinkers such as Benjamin Warfield and Abraham Kuyper. For example, Kuyper's *Lectures on Calvinism*, delivered at Princeton University, was expressly concerned with seeing Calvinism as providing a "life-system" or worldview which can provide Calvinist-Biblical answers to art, science, politics, etc., as well as counters to secularism, liberalism, etc.. See Abraham Kuyper, *Lectures on Calvinism*, (Grand Rapids, MI: Wm. B. Eerdmans Publishing, 1931). For a discussion of Van Til's relationship to the thought of Kuyper and Warfield, see Greg Bahnsen, *Van Til's Apologetic: Readings and Analysis*, (Phillipsburg, NJ: Presbyterian and Reformed Publishing, 1998), 596-609. For an example of a sustained argument against Modernism (or, in this case, Liberalism) by an early Twentieth Century Reformed thinker in the tradition of Warfield, Kuyper, and Van Til, and whose *New Testament Greek for Beginners* is still being used in seminaries today, see J. Gresham Machen, *Christianity and Liberalism*, (Grand Rapids, MI: Wm. B. Eerdmans Publishing, 1923).

[7] Though there is not room to explore it fully, one influential *Protestant* Christian response to the Enlightenment, at least as embodied in such influential figures as Kierkegaard, at least as some read him, was to turn to irrationalism, experientialism, and fideism, and to abandon the notion of a rationally defensible faith in exchange for a rationally indefensible existential faith. With his "leap of faith," Kierkegaard, apparently abandoning nearly all of Christian intellectual history perhaps together with rational human nature itself (as defined by such Church Fathers as Gregory of Nyssa and John of Damascus), denying the rational ground on which all theology (he, according to his own principles, could only irrationally affirm) was rationally developed

diverse range of options concerning the intentional choosing from a number of distinct possible apologetic methodologies, from Classical (with its strong ties to Catholic apologetic tradition, including such figures as Richard Swinburne and William Lane Craig) to Evidential (associated prominently with Gary Habermas and John Warwick Montgomery) to Reformed Epistemological (associated prominently with Alvin Plantinga) to Presuppositional (founded by Van Til) and more, and sometimes variously stressed combinations of these or others.[8] Furthermore, there are yet distinct schools of thought within

---

and articulated, and, failing to leap Lessing's *faux* ditch, held, in the words of Dulles, that "faith was ultimately irrational." See Dulles, 217-222. See also Van Til, *The Defense of the Faith*, 4th ed., ed. K. Scott Oliphant, (Phillipsburg, NJ: Presbyterian and Reformed Publishing, 2008, orig. 1955), 209-215. It was the non-Barthian Reformed counter to this phenomenon by figures such as Warfield, Kuyper, and Bavinck, realized to some degree by figures such as Van Til, Gordon Clark, and others, that helped give rise to the contemporary apologetic field *qua* field. Of course, the foregoing leaves out much, such as the work of Schleiermacher and his subjectivist notion of apologetics, the efforts of the evidentialists against historical deconstructionism, not to mention the continuous efforts of the Catholics *contra* Kant and Modernism. For 19th Century apologetic developments, see Dulles, 209-269; for the first half of 20th Century, again Dulles, 271-324. Despite being overall an invaluable work, it is however sparse and uneven in its treatment of the Patristic and Medieval eras, as well as post-1950 developments. For a fair yet critical study of Barth's destructive relationship with apologetics, see: Gordon Clark, *Karl Barth's Theological Method*, (Unicoi, TN: Trinity Foundation. 1963), 86-124. For a brief critical assessment of Kierkegaard by an apologist, see: Gordon Clark, *Thales to Dewey*, (Jefferson, MD: The Trinity Foundation, 1989), 485-492. See Appendix 2 for an apologetic critique of Lessing's Ditch.

[8] For a book-length treatment from the perspective of representative practitioners, see: *Five Views on Apologetics*, ed. Steven B. Cowan, (Grand Rapids, MI: Zondervan, 2000). For a more general, though relatively thorough, survey, see Brian K. Morley, *Mapping Apologetics: Comparing Contemporary Approaches*, (Downers Grove, IL: IVP Academic, 2015).

Irenaeus and Orthodox Apologetic Methodology

the foregoing methodologies, such that Presuppositional Apologetics as framed by Greg Bahnsen can be distinguished from that of John Frame. It can even get vitriolic, as when Van Til and Gordon Clark, who to his chagrin was counted as a type of Presuppositionalist, were at great enmity with each other apparently over their respective methodologies.[9]

It is thus into this complexity that Eastern Orthodoxy enters today, a complexity to which it also might, and arguably must, engage fruitfully and in terms developed according to its own Tradition and "within a consistent Orthodox perspective."[10] It is thus that, rather than looking, say, to Irenaeus for particular arguments against Valentinians, there is a more fruitful looking to his work for clues as to a theory of apologetics, an apologetic methodology. Considering therefore this thicket of views, the present study would like to answer, by way of illustrating the direction of study, if the text entitled *Five Views on Apologetics* were to include a sixth view, one which represents an/the Orthodox and Patristic view, what would it look like?

---

[9] For one version of this, see Herman Hoeksema, *The Clark-Van Til Controversy*, (Hobbs, NM: The Trinity Foundation, 1995). For Clark's being included among presuppositionalists (as was Francis Schaeffer), see Greg Bahnsen, *Presuppositional Apologetics: Stated and Defended*, ed. Joel McDurmon, (Powder Springs, GA: The American Vision; jointly with Nacogdoches, TX: Covenant Media Press, 2011), 137-96. For Clark's presentation of his own apologetic methodology, see Gordon Clark, *In Defense of Theology*, (Milford, MI: Mott Media, 1984).

[10] Alexander Schmemann, *For the Life of the World: Sacraments and Orthodoxy*, (Crestwood, NY: St Vladimir's Seminary Press, 1973), 117.

Irenaeus and Orthodox Apologetic Methodology

DEFINING APOLOGETICS

How, then, is the present study conceiving of apologetics? Several options for definitional sources are available, one being found in a *Dictionary of Scholastic Philosophy*:

> *apologetics, n.* the historical-philosophical explanation and defense of the presuppositions of the Christian religion, its existence, and its divine origin. Though apologetics is nowadays [1956] usually treated as a subordinate science in theology, it has been classified also as a branch of philosophy or as a part of the philosophy of religion because of its large dependence on philosophical truths and on the meaning of historical facts pertinent to religion.[11]

The above definition indicates, among other things, a view of apologetics as both an explanation and a defense, i.e. that it is a term more broad than simply referring to defense. Moreover, it also ties in the notion of philosophy which, being also in the same dictionary, is itself defined as "the science in which natural reason seeks an understanding of all things by a knowledge of their first principles."[12] As will be shown below,

---

[11] Bernard Wuellner, S. J., *Dictionary of Scholastic Philosophy*, (Fitzwilliam, NH: Loreto Publications, 2012, orig. 1956), 7-8.

[12] Wuellner, 91. Science, it is worth noting, is defined therein in philosophical contexts as "the certain intellectual knowledge of something in its causes; universal, demonstrated, organized knowledge of facts and truths and the reasons or causes of these" (ibid, 112).

the above definition of apologetics to some degree corresponds to Irenaeus' apologetic efforts.

The text *Five Views on Apologetics* defines apologetics in a general way as that discipline which "is concerned with the defense of the Christian faith against charges of falsehood, inconsistency, or credulity."[13] Honing this further, though it is an extended quote, *Five Views* further expands on the foregoing definition in key ways worth keeping in mind, as they will be useful to the present discourse as it unfolds:

> As it concerns the Christian faith, then, apologetics has to do with defending, or making a case for, the truth of the Christian faith. It is an intellectual discipline that is usually said to serve at least two purposes: (1) to bolster the faith of Christian believers, and (2) to aid in the task of evangelism. Apologists seek to accomplish these goals in two distinct ways. One is by refuting objections to the Christian faith, such as the problem of evil or the charge that Christian doctrines are incoherent. This apologetic task can be called *negative* or *defensive apologetics*. The second, perhaps complementary, way apologists fulfill their purposes is by offering positive reasons for Christian faith. The latter, called *positive* or *offensive apologetics*, often takes the form of arguments for God's existence or for the resurrection and deity of Christ but are by no means limited to these.[14]

---

[13] *Five Views on Apologetics*, 8.
[14] *Five Views*, 8.

A third definition, given by Reformed theologian John Frame in his introduction to apologetics, building his definition explicitly on 1 Peter 3:15,[15] defines apologetics generally as "the discipline that teaches Christians how to give a reason for their hope."[16] He further unpacks this in terms comprised of three distinct components: proof, defense, and offense.[17] In many ways this definition is consistent with the previous two, and a survey of apologetic literature will generally find broad definitional agreement on this level, differences largely occurring only at levels of greater specificity and application.[18] One distinct feature of Frame's definition, however, is worth mentioning, and this is his distinction between proof and offense. Whereas defense is answering to a challenge presented to Christian doctrine, and proof is providing a rational foundation for positive belief, Frame's notion of an offensive apologetic (distinct from the previous definition's use of offense) advances upon the previous definitions by indicating an outright attack on "the foolishness of unbelief," citing as support for this Psalm 14:1, 1 Corinthians 1:18-2:16, and 2 Corinthians 10:5.[19] In other words, rather than being concerned solely with answering

---

[15] "Sanctify Christ as Lord in your hearts, always being ready to make a defense (ἀπολογίαν) to everyone who asks you to give an account (λόγον) for the hope that is in you, yet with gentleness and reverence" (1Pe 3:15 NASB).

[16] John Frame, *Apologetics to the Glory of God: An Introduction*, (Phillipsburg, NJ: Presbyterian and Reformed Publishing, 1994), 1. He also footnotes here to a definition he gives in a larger work of his on Christian epistemology: "apologetics is… 'the application of Scripture to unbelief.'"

[17] Frame, *Apologetics to the Glory of God*, 2-3.

[18] See the select bibliography listing various texts on apologetics.

[19] Frame, 2-3.

incoming objections or providing reasonable grounds of credulity, this form of offense proactively seeks out to address the opponent's errors.

Further definitions of apologetics would be superfluous. One, however, and to all appearances only one, Eastern Orthodox English-language work exists that is devoted exclusively to the subject of apologetics, entitled *Orthodox Apologetic Theology*, by I. M. Andreyev, and, before moving on, his definition of apologetics is worth noting: "Orthodox Apologetics or Fundamental Theology is a theological science presenting a systematic exposition, proof and defense (apology) of the basic Christian truths as understood by the Orthodox Church."[20] Like the scholastic definition given above, Andreyev also characterizes apologetics as both systematic and scientific. It also leaves room for both the positive and negative dimensions to apologetics, though it does not seem to go as far as Frame's notion of offense. It is also noteworthy that the synonym Andreyev gives for apologetics renders it in some sense coextensive with theology.

Though the term "apologetics" is to all appearances inherited from the Western traditions, what it points to is a perennial activity of the universal Church, for the apostles and fathers of the Church have ever involved themselves in defending the faith. In this sense "apologetics," as a term, is

---

[20] I. M. Andreyev, *Orthodox Apologetic Theology*, (Platina, CA: St. Herman of Alaska Brotherhood, 1995), 45. The notion of Fundamental Theology, which Andreyev seems to hold as synonymous with apologetics, according to Dulles, emerges in the European Catholic milieu posterior to Vatican II. See Dulles, 326-8 and 338--40. This gives further credence to the notion of Catholic influence on Andreyev's conception of apologetics.

quite helpful, for it conceptually integrates these activities much as the term Christology conceptually integrates the Church's reflection on Christ, such that these can be studied and reflected on with greater clarity and depth. Andreyev's book itself, however, though presenting a beginning to the Orthodox engagement with the subject, aligned as it is (perhaps happily) with the Catholic approach, admits within that although apologetic literature is vast and diverse, "from a strictly Orthodox point of view, a fully complete, whole and deeply absorbing textbook of apologetics has not yet been prepared."[21] Unlike, say, the *Five Views* which is explicitly about *methodology*, his text cannot be said to engage with this aspect of the field of apologetics, nor with the field *as* field. More to the point, although Andreyev engages with the subject of apologetics, he does not discuss various methodologies, but engages more with arguments and positions as regards the traditional problems of apologetics, which is to say the *doing* rather than the *how*. He does discuss worldview, but being an introductory text it supplies elements of apologetic arguments, and methods of arguing them, without, however, quite getting at the underlying theory of methodology. Of course, this is not to levy blame, merely to illustrate a direction which needs to be examined, something to which the present study hopes to contribute.

    Before leaving Andreyev, a few other worthwhile observations are worth making in order to see how at least one 20th Century Orthodox philosopher-theologian perceived apologetics. Of the "science of Apologetics," he gives several

---

[21] Andreyev, 64.

designations: "Introduction to Theology, General Theology, Speculative Theology, Apologetic Theology, Encyclopedia of Theology."[22] How much weight he gives these particular terms is uncertain, but it is at least instructive to note that for him apologetics is characterized as quite broad, integrated into the whole of theology. Furthermore, echoing somewhat the scholastic definition above, he states that "this science is called the philosophy of religion, the philosophy of Christianity, the Christian conception of the world, and so forth."[23] The last, importantly, connects to the notion of worldview, which will be argued below to be a vital ingredient of Orthodox apologetics, at least as conceived by Irenaeus. As Andreyev states, "Apologetics is also a basis of the organically whole Orthodox Christian conception of the world."[24] Though this seems to contain the intuition of a methodology, the rest of Andreyev's book concerns itself largely with various apologetical problems, devoting chapters to issues such as the problem of miracles, proofs of the existence of God, and the truth of the immortality of the soul, etc.

---

[22] Ibid, 45.

[23] Ibid, 45.

[24] Ibid. In addition to reasserting the notion of a Christian worldview, and echoing elements of the expansion on the definition of apologetics given in the *Five Views* above, Andreyev also states: "Orthodox Apologetics, however, has always tried to give an intellectual synthesis of both general and particular apologetic problems, using as a cornerstone the positive method of building the organically whole Christian world-view" (Andreyev, 64). Not only, then, does Andreyev emphasize the notion of worldview, but he also sees an inherent unity between theology, philosophy, and worldview together with apologetics.

IRENAEUS OF LYONS' RELEVANCE TO APOLOGETICS

The Patristic era Father selected for the present inquiry, as indicated above, is Irenaeus of Lyons. In addition to the reasons given above, further reasons for choosing him include his being Ante-Nicene, connected to Polycarp and thus the earliest layer of Christian tradition, and also having a foundational, formative, and relatively normative status within the Eastern (and arguably Western) Churches.[25] Therefore, by focusing on his representative thought, an important step towards elucidating a normative Orthodox apologetic methodology will perhaps have been achieved. Though this in and of itself is a significant argument to hope to accomplish, this limit to only one Patristic author, however, (necessary as it is due to space constraints) renders the present thesis only a first step, a vital first step, towards a fuller elucidation of "Orthodox" apologetic methodology. The last reason is simply that Irenaeus actually does apologetics, and is moreover explicit about his apologetic motives and methods.

Of course, the above could be said to beg the question as to whether or not there even is an Orthodox apologetic methodology at all. Moreover, even if there is, there is yet the question of whether there is one primary or overarching

---

[25] Affirmations of this sort are numerous. In addition to Behr and Quasten, see also: Eric Osborn, *Irenaeus of Lyons*, (Cambridge: Cambridge University Press, 2001), xi-xiii. See also: *Irenaeus: Life, Scripture, Legacy*, eds. Sara Parvis and Paul Foster, (Minneapolis, MN: Fortress Press, 2012), 1. See also: James R. Payton, *Irenaeus on the Christian Faith: A Condensation of Against Heresies*, (Eugene, OR: Wipf & Stock Pub, 2011), 1-25.

methodology, or perhaps multiple equally compatible or incompatible methodologies. Of course, the present thesis is arguing the position that there is *at least one*, but whether or not this one is to be conceived exclusively or inclusively (for a single methodology can contain multiple methods), or as one among several, can be answered only beyond the horizons of the present study, and so is a question best asked when at least (this) one has been more or less clearly identified. As such, though the question of whether or not there are a plurality of Orthodox apologetic methodologies can only be answered in a space beyond the horizon of the present discourse, it is arguable that Irenaeus will have been established as informing, if not constituting, a Patristic baseline for normative Orthodox apologetics.[26]

That said, as this study is within the field of systematics, it will also not be concerned with, for example, Irenaeus' reception history, which is to say whether or not his apologetic efforts are picked up in an explicit manner by others. Beyond the affirmation of his great authority as perhaps the pre-eminent canonical Ante-Nicene theologian (which otherwise might have gone to Origen), with connections via Polycarp to the earliest strata of Christian tradition, the appropriation or non-appropriation of his methodology by others falls outside the scope of the present study, though it might be mentioned that even a cursory study of Origen's *Contra Celsum*, for example, will show that the methodological thoroughness and attention to detail found in Irenaeus is also

---

[26] See Appendix 1 for a preliminary evaluation of the apologetic methodology discernable within the works of both Athanasius and Gregory of Nyssa.

present there.[27] The same restriction of interest to methodology rather than to reception history applies equally to Irenaeus' theology, which is presupposed for the purposes of the present study.[28] One word concerning Irenaeus' importance, however, seems appropriate. As Irenaeus scholar John Behr states:

> "Standing at the very foundation of all the diverse forms of Christianity we see today, Irenaeus must be read with all due diligence and seriousness, whether one regards his work negatively or positively. This is, moreover, not simply an exercise of history but a necessary task of the work of understanding Christian identity today. ... Irenaeus has... never been more contemporary and important."[29]

In order to draw out Irenaeus' relevance for the sake of apologetics, the present study will take an exegetical look at key sections of his works. Following this the study will turn its attention to examining its findings in light of the contemporary field of apologetics, also drawing on Irenaean themes such as *hypothesis* and the canon of truth. Then the study will briefly

---

[27] Quasten states that "Irenaeus is by far the most important of the theologians of the second century," and, what is more, "deserves to be called the founder of Christian theology... the first to formulate in dogmatic terms the entire Christian doctrine" (Quasten, 287, 294). If Quasten is right in his assessment, it is all the more remarkable considering that this is founded in large part on his apologetic efforts.

[28] Further in the study, however, there will be a discussion concerning his "theological methodology" and the manner in which it informs his apologetic methodology.

[29] John Behr, *Irenaeus of Lyons: Identifying Christianity*, (Oxford: Oxford University Press, 2013), 1.

evaluate one major contemporary Orthodox theologian's apologetics so as to both set in relief some of the dynamics of Orthodox apologetic methodology as argued herein and indicate how this can also be used as a tool for evaluating other Orthodox apologetic efforts. Without an understanding of this dimension of the Church's perennial activity, and without being informed by the efforts of foundational Church Fathers such as Irenaeus, the likelihood of operating blindly and ineffectually is dramatically increased, greatly reducing the ability of the Church to defend itself from error both within and without. By uncovering Irenaeus' apologetic methodology, however, a fuller and more complete approach to apologetics can be established critically and on solid ground, one which takes strength from the fullness of the Church's timeless living tradition.

THE IRENAEAN EVIDENCE: AN EXPOSITION IN LIGHT OF APOLOGETICS

What, then, is Irenaeus' apologetic methodology? Does Irenaeus provide the substance of an Orthodox Christian apologetic methodology? What are some of the proffered frameworks of motive and method which he gives? Of his extant works, in order to discover Irenaeus' conception of apologetic methodology, as well as the motives innervating it and the methods instantiating it, the prefaces and conclusions of the *Demonstration of the Apostolic Preaching* and each of the five books of the *Adversus Haereses* will be the objects of study. As will be seen, Irenaeus is quite forthright in these texts about the *scopos*

Irenaeus and Orthodox Apologetic Methodology

of his apologetical efforts, and as such they will serve to orient the present study. The following expositions, it might be noted, are intended to be indicative, with a more synthetic assessment of the findings following after the present section.

Demonstration of the Apostolic Preaching[30]

Irenaeus is clear at the beginning of his *Demonstration of the Apostolic Preaching* as to why he is doing apologetics. As Quasten observes, the very title, which incorporates the term "demonstration" (*ἐπίδειξις*), suggests that it is an "apologetic treatise."[31] Moreover, within the text itself apologetics is given as one of the motives of this summary demonstration of the truth, for as Irenaeus states, "We are sending you, as it were, a summary memorandum, so that… you may confound all those who hold false opinions."[32] In other words, Irenaeus is motivated

---

[30] Irenaeus of Lyons, *On the Apostolic Preaching*, tr. John Behr, (Crestwood, NY: St Vladimir's Seminary Press, 1997).

[31] Quasten, 292.

[32] *Demonstration of the Apostolic Preaching*, 1. See also Quasten, 292. Behr is correct in the introductory remarks to his translation when he states that Irenaeus' *Demonstration* is "presented in a non-polemical or apologetic *manner*" (Behr, *Dem.* 7) (emphasis added). It is, however, a meaningful distinction to identify what is apologetical in "manner" and what is apologetical in "nature." Irenaeus is clear in his opening paragraph that his "summary memorandum" is intended "so that… you may confound all those who hold false opinions." Thus, whether or not it is written in an apologetic "manner" cannot be determinative of whether or not apologetics is, in a manner of speaking, enfolded in the text, for in this case Irenaeus is unambiguous about this intention. The question, moreover, as to what constitutes an apologetic

in writing so that those to whom he entrusts this work will be enabled to stop those who hold false opinions.

Notice that at this point he does not suggest that his reader immediately seek to "persuade" those who hold false opinions. Rather, the group who holds false opinions are not treated as innocently misguided, but as needing to be confounded, stopped, silenced.[33] As will be shown below, the notion of persuasion only follows upon a prior refutation. For everyone, however, "who desires to know," he says his work may be used to "deliver our sound and irreproachable word in all boldness." This group is marked as having a desire to know, but the group which holds to false opinions, these are simply to be confounded.

What, however, is at stake? Irenaeus is not silent: "The ways of those who do not see are many, dark and divergent… [leading] down to death, separating man from God."[34] Thus it is shown that, according to Irenaeus, a motivation to apologetics is rooted in the consequences attending upon the divergent paths one might take. The first, which leads to the kingdom and to unity with God, is safeguarded by apologetics, for it confounds those who lead others away from the path of life, protecting those who might be misled by those who "do not see," who might grow slack, fall into error, and thereby wander

---

manner needs to be clarified, something which the present section hopes in some measure to accomplish.

[33] To connect this Irenaean thought to Pauline language: "We destroy arguments and every lofty opinion raised against the knowledge of God, and take every thought captive to obey Christ" (2 Co 10:5). Similarly: "I say this in order that no one may delude you with plausible arguments" (Col 2:4).

[34] *Dem.* 1.

into death: "Thus it is necessary for you and for all who are concerned about their salvation to make [your] way by faith, without deviation, surely and resolutely, lest, in slacking, you remain in gross desires, or, erring, wander from the right [path]." Apologetics, therefore, is conceived as an enterprise protective of the faithful, keeping them from taking false paths.

Irenaeus, in the same section, expositing the first psalm, concludes by saying that "the pestilential are those who pervert not only themselves, but others also, by evil and twisted teaching... and such are all heretics, they sit 'in the chair of the pestilential' and [corrupt] those who receive the poison of their teaching."[35] Again apologetics is seen to play a protective role, guarding those who can be made to wander according to the dictates of false teachers and their false teaching. In order to do this, it also means that a primary task of apologetics is to reveal error, an issue which, it will be seen, Irenaeus is explicit about. At this point, however, there is at least this strong awareness that false teaching can pervert and poison the people it misleads. In short, ideas have consequences.

Apologetics is therefore motivated to defend and stabilize both true doctrine and the people who would both keep it and be kept by it, for "lest we suffer any such thing, we must keep the rule of faith unswervingly, and perform the commandments of God," for if true doctrine gets corrupted, the tie that binds faith and action will be severed, and people will be unable to practice the truth. As such, it is apologetics which functions to keep this doctrine pure for the sake of the exercise

---

[35] *Dem.* 2.

of faith. As Irenaeus states: "Action, then, comes by faith... and the truth brings about faith, for faith is established upon things truly real, that we may believe what really is, as it is, and [believing] what really is, as it is, we may also keep our conviction of it firm."[36] Thus apologetics is motivated to keep the faithful standing in the light of reality, maintaining the truth, as it is, so that faith can be brought about and established firmly, and so that this faith, brought about by truth, can produce right action.

Irenaeus concludes his preface: "Since, then, the conserver (συνεκτικός) of our salvation is faith, it is necessary to take great care of it, that we may have a true comprehension of what is."[37] Thus there is an irremovable motive to apologetics, for its job is to defend, maintain, and clarify saving faith in opposition to deathly error. Since faith is that which "conserves" salvation, that which defends the faith, which is to say apologetics, is therefore also a necessary part of the Christian faith itself as understood by Irenaeus. As such, since according to Irenaeus it is necessary to take great care of the truth of this faith, it is therefore likewise necessary to do apologetics with great care in order to make this happen, in order to maintain a right comprehension of what this faith's saving truth is.

From the foregoing it is possible, and arguably proper, to view the *Demonstration of the Apostolic Preaching* as a textbook summary for (which is not necessarily to say "of") apologetics. As was noted above, the *Demonstration* is self-reportedly

---

[36] *Dem.* 3.
[37] *Dem.* 3.

intended to equip his audience for an apologetic task, that of confounding those who speak falsehood. Though the *Demonstration* is not itself directly "defensive," or, to use another of the terms from the definitions above, negative, its construction is yet explicitly framed as aimed at and oriented towards equipping the apologetic effort, and so in itself models the positive or constructive side of apologetics.[38] In this light, the *Demonstration* also falls well within the scope of Andreyev's definition, for Irenaeus is presenting a "systematic exposition [and] proof... of the basic Christian truths as understood by the Orthodox Church."[39] By demonstrating the apostolic preaching of the truth and establishing his arguments rationally on first principles and according to a systematic exposition of Scriptural proofs, Irenaeus places his work squarely within the realm of apologetics.[40]

Concerning methodology, as noted above, the very word "demonstration" (επίδειξιν), which is at the very least evocative of Greek philosophical usage, points towards a

---

[38] Quasten makes a useful distinction consistent with the various dimensions of apologetics noted in the above definitions that, having "no polemical part," the *Demonstration* is "limited to a positive proof." See Quasten, 292-3.

[39] Andreyev, *Orthodox Apologetic Theology*, 45.

[40] The term systematic, as will be argued more fully below, is understood in this context as indicating, most fundamentally, an intention towards an orderly and internally coherent account. At the very least, by establishing his *Demonstration* theologically on the framework of the Trinitarian Baptismal formula, "the order of our faith"(*Dem.* 6), in 1-7, and then generally following a "history of salvation" scheme followed by what might be roughly understood as a manual of prophetic proofs, Irenaeus has conformed himself to the general notion of "systematic." For more discussion of Irenaeus' structure, see also James Wiegel, *The Trinitarian Structure of Irenaeus' Demonstration of the Apostolic Preaching*, (SVTQ vol. 58.2).

particular branch of reasoned argumentation which, at least according to Aristotle in his *Topics*, produces conclusions which "necessarily" (ἀνάγκης) follow from "true and primary" (ἀληθῶν καί πρώτων) premises which he likewise calls ἀπόδειξις.[41] At the very least, rationality is implied and intended, and though the scope of the present study does not allow for an extensive look at the entire text of Irenaeus' *Demonstration*, before looking to his conclusion it is noteworthy concerning "demonstration" that in the opening of part one, right after discussing the saving nature of faith and how baptism into this faith is a "rebirth unto God," Irenaeus argues first for the existence of God, and moreover derives from this the fittingness for a foundation of faith:

> For it is necessary that things that have come into being have received the origin of their being (ἀρχή γενέσεως) from some great cause; and the origin of all is God, for He Himself was not made by anyone, but everything was made by Him. And therefore it is proper, first of all, to believe that there is one God, the Father, who has created and fashioned all things, who made that which was not to be, who contains all and who alone is uncontainable.[42]

---

[41] In Book 1 Part 1 of *Topics*, Aristotle defines a demonstration: "Now reasoning is an argument in which, certain things being laid down, something other than these necessarily comes about through them. (a) It is a 'demonstration' [ἀπόδειξις], when the premises from which the reasoning starts are true and primary, or are such that our knowledge of them has originally come through premises which are primary and true" (*Topics*, 100a.25-30).

[42] *Dem.* 4.

Since according to Irenaeus being must have an originating cause, according to him it is in this sense also proper to begin with this originating cause as the true and primary starting point of both faith and faith's demonstration. It is precisely in demonstrating from this that he can be said to draw the conclusion about Christianity's first metaphysical premise for, "in this way, then, it is demonstrated [that there is] One God."[43] Since, then, God is the origin of being, which is to say all being has its derivation from Him as from "some great cause," it is therefore fitting to take God as the foundation or starting point of faith. Thus Irenaeus can be said to be engaging in rational demonstration from first principles, which is also to say that his notion of faith implies a methodological commitment to reason and rational argumentation which, not incidentally, enables and informs his practice of apologetics.[44] Beginning with being, Irenaeus argues it is "necessary" for the "things that have come into being" that they have a singular "great cause." The very notion of a primary, originating "great cause" related to the notion of being is also evocative of Aristotelian thought, and even if it cannot be demonstrated that he directly derives this from Aristotle or one of his commentators, Irenaeus' treating this as a necessary principle makes it yet clear that *demonstration*, reasoned proof, is intended: "In this way, then, it

---

[43] *Dem.* 5. Beginning his demonstration thus, it is only *after* this that Irenaeus demonstrates the Word and the Spirit.

[44] Cf. Aristotle, *Topics* Book I:100a:25-6: "reasoning is an argument (ἔστι δή συλλογισμός λόγος) in which, certain things being laid down, something other than these necessarily (ἀνάγκης) comes about through them."

is *demonstrated* [δείκνυται] [that there is] One God, the Father, uncreated, invisible, Creator of all, above whom there is no other God, and after whom there is no other God."[45] Irenaeus thus establishes his metaphysical First Principle, his "necessary" and essential premise, the one from which to methodologically build the rest of his positive demonstration, and as such it is from this true and primary premise that the rest of the demonstration of the apostolic preaching flows.

The conclusion of the *Demonstration* substantiates the claim of an apologetic dimension and orientation via its symmetrical recapitulation of the first sections' observation concerning the grave seriousness of error.[46] Irenaeus states in the conclusion to his *Demonstration* that "error... has caused much straying from the truth... And we must be wary of all such

---

[45] *Dem.* 5. In a section dealing with the Irenaean notion of *hypothesis* and its connect to canon, Behr also makes a connection with Aristotle while making reference to the concept of demonstration. See Behr, *Irenaeus*, 112.

[46] *Dem.* 99-100. Behr notes in his translation that there is a challenge to the claim that the last two paragraphs (99-100) of the *Demonstration* may be attributed to a later editor. (See note 229 on page 118.) Two of the supporting arguments he gives for this are 1) "the unique manner of translating a Greek genitive absolute at the beginning of *Dem.* 99," and 2) "the atypical use of the term 'seal' as an equivalent of baptism." Of the first claim, certainly a unique grammatical construction does not decide the case, as this could be attributed to other factors. Concerning the second claim, however, the term "seal" presents itself also at the beginning of the work, as Behr also notes. (See note 13 on 102.) Irenaeus states at the beginning: "this baptism is the seal (σφραγίς) of eternal life"(DAP, 3), and at the end: "error, concerning the three heads of our seal"(DAP, 99). Thus, being at both the beginning and the end, and in both places referring to the Trinitarian substance of baptism, the notion of "seal" therefore serves to actually support rather than undermine the idea that the conclusion is of a unity with the entire work.

and flee from their thought."[47] Thus Irenaeus maintains that the preceding sections fit in with the scope as established in the beginning, that the motive of his apologetics is oriented towards confounding errors and keeping "the rule of faith unswervingly."[48] Thus Irenaeus portrays that his apologetics is motivated towards both a "negative" end, that of confounding heretics, and a "positive" end, that of strengthening the faithful in their maintenance of the truth.[49] Thus, "it is necessary to keep with all strictness" this truth and, as such, there is a perennial and necessary motivation to perform apologetics in order to strictly keep the purity of this preaching.[50]

Adversus Haereses, or The Exposure and Refutation of Knowledge Falsely So-Called[51]

---

[47] *Dem.* 100.

[48] *Dem.* 2.

[49] It is noteworthy that there is no immediate appeal to persuading anyone, indicating that there is not an overriding "rhetorical" purpose to the *Demonstration*, rhetoric being understood as motivated towards persuasion.

[50] *Dem.* 98.

[51] Latin and Greek source citations of Irenaeus' *Adversus Haereses* (*AH*) will be drawn from: Saint Irenaeus, Bishop of Lyon, *Libros Quinque Adversus Haereses*, 2

Irenaeus and Orthodox Apologetic Methodology

Book I

Unlike the apologetical methodology of Irenaeus' *Demonstration*, composed as it was of a more exclusively positive construction, his magnum opus against the heresies, however, is constituted of both positive and negative proof. Looking at his *Adversus Haereses* for indications of a motive to apologetics, in Book I he gives a succinct description of his motive:

> Inasmuch as certain men have set the truth aside, and bring in lying words and vain genealogies... and by means of their craftily-constructed plausibilities (πανούργως συγκεκροτημένης πιθανότητος, *subdole exercitata verisimilitudo*) draw away the minds of the inexperienced and take them captive, I have felt constrained, my dear friend, to compose the following treatise in order to expose and counteract their machinations.[52]

With allusions to Scripture, particularly Titus 3:9's mention of genealogies, Irenaeus here states that his motivation is to "expose and counteract" that which appears true but is not. He

---

vols. ed. W. Harvey, (Cantabrigiae: Typis academicis, 1857). There is yet to be a complete English translation since that found in *Ante-Nicene Fathers*, Vol. 1. ed. Alexander Roberts, James Donaldson, and A. Cleveland Coxe, (Buffalo, NY: Christian Literature Publishing Co., 1885). For consistency of idiom, this translation will be utilized, with regular reference to the source languages to ensure a minimum of semantic distortion.

[52] *AH*, Pref. I.1. Cf. Col 2:4: "I say this in order that no one may delude you with plausible arguments."

notes that they are subtle in their lies (*verba falsa*), crafty in their machinations, and that those who set the truth aside "draw away the mind" of the simpler and less experienced among the faithful. These deceptions actually take people "captive," and so he is compelled to do apologetics in order to stop this from happening.[53] Apologetics is thus protective, for "they also overthrow the faith of many, by drawing them away, under a pretence of superior knowledge."[54] Apologetics in this sense is motivated by a war against the subtleties of false knowledge.

> Concerning the nature of error, Irenaeus continues:
> Error, indeed, is never set forth in its naked deformity, lest, being thus exposed, it should at once be detected. But it is craftily decked out in an attractive dress, so as, by its outward form, to make it appear to the inexperienced (ridiculous as the expression may seem) more true than the truth itself.[55]

From the foregoing it is clear that Irenaeus is motivated by a certain view of the nature of error. In his view it is inherently self-obscuring, self-concealing, and "never set forth in its naked deformity." It even has a certain intrinsic dynamic to remain hidden, "lest, being exposed, it should at once be detected." Thus it requires an intellectual effort to address, or to continue Irenaeus' metaphor, to undress, error. As Behr notes, "a

---

[53] Concerning captivity language: Cf. 2Co 10:5: "We destroy arguments and every lofty opinion raised against the knowledge of God, and take every thought captive to obey Christ."
[54] *AH*, Pref. I.1.
[55] *AH*, Pref. I.2.

refutation by exposure," to expose the error is therefore to dispose the error, thus beginning the process of eradication by revealing that which would remain concealed.[56] Motivation unto apologetics is thus given shape by the nature of error, and as such the protective motive for apologetics in turn motivates, if not militates, the methodology of revealing purported error.

Since error is "craftily decked out in an attractive dress," it can therefore be understood that skill and even dispassion is involved in its detection, for one must be both knowledgeable enough to detect it and dispassionate enough not to be lured by its attractiveness. As such, in order to protect the "inexperienced," Irenaeus' apologetic must actually do battle with the perceived error, for it will continue to deceive "unless it come under the eye of one able to test and expose the counterfeit."[57] Because, then, the vulnerably inexperienced are always present in the Church, Irenaeus states about the necessity of not failing to do apologetics:

> Lest, therefore, through my neglect, some should be carried off, even as sheep are by wolves, while they perceive not the true character of these men,— because they outwardly are covered with sheep's clothing... and because their language resembles ours, while their sentiments are very different—I have deemed it my duty (after reading some of the *Commentaries*, as they call them, of the disciples of Valentinus, and after making myself acquainted with their tenets through personal intercourse with some of them) to unfold to

---

[56] Behr, *Irenaeus of Lyons*, 75.
[57] *AH*, Pref. I.2.

you, my friend, these portentous and profound mysteries, which do not fall within the range of every intellect, because all have not sufficiently purged their brains.[58]

The foregoing paragraph clearly delineates important dimensions to Irenaeus' motives, and reinforces the idea that certain apologetic methodologies emerge as a consequence of these motives. Again it is clear that the will to protect is key among Irenaeus' motives, for he recognizes that intellectual subtleties "do not fall within the range" of untrained intellects (*quae non omnes capiunt, quia non omnes cerebrum habent*), indicating the sophisticated and intellectual nature of apologetics, and that intellectual training is prejacent to its practice. Moreover, the very subtlety of the error motivates him, for error can masquerade as truth, can be "outwardly... covered with sheep's clothing." Thus he seeks to distinguish between familial language and foreign sentiments, to unmask or unfold that which is hidden.

This notion of exposing that which is hidden, unfolding that which is enfolded in plausible language, then, points to a case for *systems methodology*, which is to say a particular form of critical analysis and argumentation which does not operate merely at the level of claim-counterclaim but instead aims at the presuppositions and structures of entire systems for, as Irenaeus

---

[58] *AH*, Pref. I.2. In the omitted portion of this citation is a reference to the Lord's command to be on guard against such: "Beware of the false prophets, who come to you in sheep's clothing, but inwardly are ravenous wolves" (Mat 7:15). Irenaeus seems to understand this as a command, one which has important implications for apologetics.

indicates, the claims may outwardly appear as sheep. As such, Irenaeus seeks to familiarize himself with their tenets with the express purpose of unmasking the entire enemy system (*omnem regulam*),[59] the phony discourse which seeks to insinuate itself among the faithful and thereby deceive and misguide them.[60]

Thus Irenaeus' apologetics is motivated by an apperception of the principle truth claims implicit in whole systems of thought and which lay, in a manner of speaking, "behind" any rhetorical appearance, what Irenaeus above called error's "outward form" which speciously approximates the canon of truth and as such needs to be exposed. In the language of Irenaeus' metaphor, the wolf which lies enfolded in the skin of the sheep causes itself to look like a sheep while all the while moving and motivated according to the concealed predisposition of a wolf.[61] A motivation to apologetics, in this

---

[59] *AH*, Pref. II.2.

[60] As will be argued more fully below, the connection of *regulam* with "system" is founded on the intrinsic and immanent relationship between a system of thought and its *regulam* such that, to speak of the *omnem regulam* is, by by necessary implication, to speak of the whole system. Hefner's study of Irenaeus' theological methodology supports this Irenaean notion of system. See: Philip Hefner, "Theological Methodology and St. Irenaeus," The Journal of Religion, Vol. 44, No. 4 (Oct., 1964), pp. 294-309. For example, he argues: "The one highest authority for Irenaeus is the system, framework, or 'hypothesis' of the Faith." See: Hefner, 295.

[61] In other words, as a wolf masquerading in sheep clothing does not "say" it is a wolf, likewise a heresy will not "say" it is a heresy, and, more realistically, it will not say it is denying or seeking to deny orthodox truth claims. In fact, it may be persuaded that it is in fact a sheep, which is to say, rightful. For example, one who argues on behalf of Sophiology would not say they are undermining Orthodox Trinitarian discourse, and as such they will outwardly affirm orthodoxy. As such, and implicit in Irenaeus' whole-systems methodology against heresy, it is the duty of apologists to go behind the

sense, thus itself motivates unto a presuppositional or systems methodology, a motive to do apologetics in a certain way, i.e. to go behind error's "outward form" so as to reveal or unfold the predisposition or presupposition (i.e. *hypothesis*) which is enfolded in the error's whole system of discourse.[62]

Irenaeus is clear about another dimension of his motive: "I do this, in order that you, obtaining an acquaintance with these things, may in turn explain them to all those with whom you are connected, and exhort them to avoid such an abyss of madness and of blasphemy against Christ."[63] In other words, in addition to his protective spirit, Irenaeus is further showing that his apologetics is motivated by a pedagogical intention, so that the reader "may in turn explain" that which he is unfolding, and thus it is not restricted to a few individuals, but to "all those with whom you are connected," the trained and untrained, i.e. so that those in the Church can be enabled to avoid error. Moreover, he wants his reader to "expand (*auges*) those ideas" of which he sends "only the seminal principles" (*semen*), and with comprehensive understanding to develop

---

surface claims, behind the surface affirmation of "orthodoxy," and therein integrally exegete the consequences of its conceptual grammar, explicate its presuppositions, and then to affirm or deny holistically, which is to say systematically, on this basis. Accordingly, apologetics might be viewed as "dialectical intersystematics," a type of critical systems analysis.

[62] Recalling Behr's discussion, noted above, concerning the Irenaean notion of *hypothesis* and its vital connection with the notion of *canon*, it is worthwhile to note that, coming from the Greek, *hypothesis* is closely allied if not synonymous with the etymologically Latin term *presupposition*. From this vantage, so-called presuppositional apologetics could find a distinctly Orthodox construction, one deeply informed by the Irenaean notion of *canon*.

[63] *AH*, pref. I.2.

these points "to their full extent" (*et in latitudine sensus tui in multum fructificabis ea*).[64] Irenaeus thus intends an ongoing development of his apologetic thought. Almost as if inculcating a culture of apologetics, apologetics in Irenaeus' thought thus also has an especially intra-ecclesial focus, which also implies that it is aimed primarily at *informing* "insiders" rather than persuading either opponents or outsiders. This is not to say that he is intending secrecy, nor even that his opponents are to be shielded from his arguments, or that persuasion is forbidden, but that the intended *audience* of Irenaeus' apologetic discourse is first the Church. It is motivated by a desire to protect the faithful in their maintenance of both truth's doctrine and practice. Moreover, it is a platform for exhortation against an "abyss of madness and... blasphemy."[65] In other words, the preservation of the good name of Christ also plays a central role motivating Irenaeus' practice of apologetics.

Regarding his apologetic methodology, Irenaeus states that he intends according to his ability, "with brevity and clearness to set forth (*docent*) the opinions (*sententiam*)" of the

---

[64] *AH*, pref. I.3.

[65] Though there is not space in the present study to explore this relatively common theme concerning the relationship between heresy and madness, rather than reducing said notion to hyperbole or anachronistically translating it into a reference to contemporary psychiatric designations, if one conceptualizes sanity as the mode of life and reasoning founded on truth, believing "what really is, as it is" (*Dem.* 3), and madness as the mode of life and reasoning founded on folly, as becoming "broken and spoilt, not being whole, when falseness enters the soul" (*Dem.* 2), then the statement can be read as simply descriptive of that consequence which flows from a series of erroneous ethical and metaphysical commitments. The antithesis to this, according to Irenaeus, is that a person will be "preserved in beauty and due measure, when truth is continually in the soul and holiness in the body."

heretics and their school (*scholae*).[66] What he further seeks to accomplish is "to furnish the means of overthrowing (ἀνατρέπειν) them, by showing how absurd and inconsistent with the truth are their statements."[67] Thus Irenaeus' apologetic method is one of setting forth the false rule or pattern (*regulam*) of doctrine and showing how it is inconsistent with the truth. It is a getting inside the heretical school's thought-system and deconstructing the ground on which it stands by unmasking and setting forth its absurdity and its inconsistency, and it is his "feeling of affection which prompts" him to bring this to light, to make known "those doctrines which have been kept in concealment."[68] With a clear and unwavering eye towards that which would otherwise seek to remain concealed, he summarizes this at the end of the preface when he states that he "spared no pains, not only to make these doctrines known (*non solum facere tibi manifestam*)... but also to furnish the means of showing their falsity (*sed et subministrationem dare, uti ostenderemus eam falsam*)... that men may no longer be drawn away (*abstrahantur*) by the plausible system (*ab illorum suadela*) of these heretics."[69] This two-pronged approach, then, is that of critical examination *cum* exposure together with overthrowal of the plausible system in order to protect the faithful. Moreover, not merely offering fish, Irenaeus also expresses the compassionate wish that his audience learn to fish, which is to say expand on that which he merely furnishes as a beginning,

---

[66] *AH*, pref. I.2.
[67] *AH*, pref. I.2.
[68] *AH*, pref. I.2.
[69] *AH*, pref. I.3.

hinting at the traditioning of a system of apologetics, a system of which Irenaeus supplies the rudiments.

One further feature of Irenaeus' apologetic worth mentioning is a type of stylistic self-abnegation: "Thou wilt not expect from me... any display of rhetoric... or any excellence of composition... or any beauty or persuasiveness of style, to which I make no pretensions."[70] Taking Irenaeus at his word, this would not be merely a phony humility, but an intentional approach towards apologetics. In a sense it is characteristic of Christian apologetics. For example, John of Damascus, though known for his eloquence, makes a similar appeal in his first treatise against the iconoclasts: "receive my discourse with kindness, paying no attention to my little worth, nor expecting eloquence in my words... but rather considering the power of my arguments."[71] With language echoing that of 1 Corinthians 2:4-5, John of Damascus is actually highlighting the power of argumentation by asking that it be considered apart from rhetorical flourish and stylistic nuance.[72] In support of this he appeals perhaps surprisingly to 1 Corinthians 4:20: "For the kingdom of God does not consist in words (λόγῳ) but in power (δυνάμει)." In this reading it is precisely the *argument*, the *force* of reason rather than some slick eloquence, which has power. Irenaeus, in making this type of appeal, likewise draws

---

[70] *AH*, pref. I.3.

[71] John of Damascus, *Three Treatises on the Divine Images*, tr. Andrew Louth, (Crestwood: St. Vladimir's Seminary Press, 2003), I.3.

[72] "and my message and my preaching were not in persuasive words of wisdom, but in demonstration of the Spirit and of power, so that your faith would not rest on the wisdom of men, but on the power of God" (1Co 2:4-5).

attention above all to his argumentation. He, like Damascene does much later, moreover appeals to his readers that they receive and accept his discourse "in a kindly spirit," what he has written "simply, truthfully, and in [his own] homely way."[73] In this light, the appeal to simplicity and non-rhetoricality of style is thus not a retreat from reasoned argumentation but from vain flourish. It sets in relief the fact of the centrality of reasoned argumentation.[74]

At the end of Book I, Irenaeus returns to discuss his methodology, this time incorporating "the hope that perchance some of them, exercising repentance and returning to the only Creator… may obtain salvation."[75] Clearly, then, the defeat of their error includes the *possibility* for a correction of those in error, but it could not be said that this possibility defines his efforts for, that said, Irenaeus returns to his intra-ecclesial intention: "that others may not henceforth be drawn away by

---

[73] *AH*, pref. I.3.

[74] Though there is not space to enter into the debate here, there is what can only be called a certain *rhetoromania* common to certain forms of subjectivism which reads everything as rhetorical to the degree that all appeal to non-rhetoricality is simply a psychological subterfuge which in a backhanded way is "really" highlighting rhetoricality such that all other considerations of truth are mitigated, marginalized, and subsumed under the rubric of persuasion, a mere posing for the sake of *ethos*. It stands to reason, however, that Irenaeus is being quite forthright about writing "simply, truthfully, and in a homely way." Kreeft, in his *Handbook of Christian Apologetics*, makes a key distinction between logical and psychological certainty: "Psychological certainty is what we call *certitude*: a *feeling* of certainty. And this is not what we mean by the certainty that belongs to a solid demonstration" (Peter Kreeft, *Handbook of Christian Apologetics*, (Downers Grove, IL: IVP, 1994), 19).

[75] *AH*, XXXI.3.

their wicked, although plausible, persuasions."[76] To protect and equip his flock most effectively against the wolves, he found it "was necessary clearly to prove, that, as their very opinions and regulations exhibit them," they are in self-refuting error.[77] Refutation, then, and not persuasion, is his primary guiding principle here. Moreover, he wants the faithful to "look with contempt (*derideant*) upon their doctrines (*doctrinam*)."[78] It is apparently not enough to disagree neutrally but, with mercy for those beset by this ignorance, to hate that ignorance by which they are beset.[79] Hating their error, Irenaeus is yet clear about the need the faithful have to pity those in error:

> ... pity (*misereantur*) those who, still cleaving to these miserable (*miserrimis*) and baseless (*instabilibus*) fables, have reached such a pitch of arrogance as to reckon themselves superior to all others on account of such

---

[76] *AH*, XXXI.3. *Reliqui autem non jam abstrahantur a prava quasi verisimili suasione eorum.*

[77] *AH*, XXXI.3.

[78] *AH*, XXXI.3.

[79] This is also a pervasive biblical theme. Cf. "The fear of the LORD is to hate evil; pride and arrogance and the evil way and the perverted mouth, I hate" (Pro 8:13). "The fear of the LORD is to hate evil; Pride and arrogance and the evil way And the perverted mouth, I hate" (Pro 8:13). "Hate evil, you who love the LORD, Who preserves the souls of His godly ones; He delivers them from the hand of the wicked" (Psa 97:10). "I will set no worthless thing before my eyes; I hate the work of those who fall away; It shall not fasten its grip on me" (Psa 101:3). "From Your precepts I get understanding; Therefore I hate every false way" ... "Therefore I esteem right all Your precepts concerning everything, I hate every false way" (Psa 119:104, 128). "Hate evil, love good, And establish justice in the gate! Perhaps the LORD God of hosts May be gracious to the remnant of Joseph" (Amo 5:15). "Let love be without hypocrisy. Abhor what is evil; cling to what is good" (Rom 12:9).

knowledge (*agnitionem*), or, as it should be called, ignorance (*ignorantium*).[80]

Thus there is inculcated a dialectic tension between, on the one hand, a sense of mercy and love towards persons in error together with, on the other hand, a simultaneous hatred of their error. This is followed up by Irenaeus with a conclusion reinforcing his methodological presupposition: "They have now been fully exposed; and simply to exhibit their sentiments (*sententiae*), is to obtain a victory (*victoria*) over them."[81] This method of exposure unto destruction is then given one of Irenaeus' fullest treatments in the last paragraph at the end of Book I. Though it is a long quote, it is vital for understanding Irenaeus' conception of apologetic methodology.

> Wherefore I have laboured (*conati*) to bring forward, and make clearly manifest (*facere manifestum*), the utterly ill-conditioned carcass of this miserable little fox.[82] For there will not now be need of many words (*sermonibus*) to overturn their system of doctrine (*evertendum doctrinam eorum*), when it has been made manifest to all (*manifestam omnibus factam*). It is as when, on a beast hiding itself in a wood, and by rushing forth from it is in the habit of destroying multitudes (*multos vastantis*), one who beats round the wood and thoroughly explores it (*denudat*), so as to compel the

---

[80] *AH*, XXXI.3.
[81] *AH*, XXXI.3.
[82] *Quapropter conati sumus nos universum male compositum vulpeculae hujus corpusculum in medium producere, et aperte facere manifestum.*

animal to break cover (*segregat*), does not strive to capture it, seeing that it is truly a ferocious (*fera fera*) beast; but those present can then watch and avoid its assaults, and can cast darts at it from all sides (*jaculari undique*), and wound (*vulnerare*) it, and finally slay that destructive brute (*interficere vastatricem illam bestiam*). So, in our case, since we have brought their hidden mysteries (*manifestum redegerimus eorum abscondita*), which they keep in silence among themselves (*abscondita et apud se tacita mysteria*), to the light, it will not now be necessary to use many words in destroying (*destruere*) their system of opinions (*sententiam*).[83] ... Since then the case is so, I shall, according to promise, and as my ability serves, labour to overthrow (*eversionem*) them, by refuting (*contradicentes*) them all in the following book. Even to give an account of them is a tedious affair, as you see (*ennaratio enim in longum pergit, ut vides*). But I shall furnish means (*viatica quoque dabimus*) for overthrowing (*eversionem*) them, by meeting all their opinions in the order in which they have been described (*secundum narrationis ordinem*), that I may not only expose (*ostendentes*) the wild beast to view, but may inflict wounds (*vulnerantes*) upon it from every side (*undique*).[84]

---

[83] *Sic et nobis, cum in manifestum redegerimus eorum abscondita et apud se tacita mysteria, jam non erit necessarium multis destruere eorum sententiam.*
[84] *AH*, XXXI.4.

Irenaeus and Orthodox Apologetic Methodology

In the above, Irenaeus not only admits to the extensive nature of even the setting-up portion of the apologetic task, but he also determines to thoroughly meet all their opinions so as to wound their false system of doctrine from every side.[85] Nothing short of total destruction, then, is the methodological aim of his apologetic task. Nothing can be left for the false doctrine to stand on. According to his analogy with the wounding of the destructive and wild beast (*bestiam*), it is from all sides that the darts are to be thrown, and not only by him. Apologetics as conceived by Irenaeus is thus a universally relevant task, one he is traditioning to the Church even if many are not able to personally cast darts: "For it is now in your power, and in the power of all your associates, to familiarize (*exerceri*) yourselves with what has been said, to overthrow (*evertere*) their wicked (*nequam*) and undigested (*inconditas*) doctrines (*doctrinas*), and to set forth doctrines (*dogmata*) agreeable to the truth (*veritati*)."[86]

Book II

In the preface of the second book, Irenaeus is even more careful to express how labored and detailed is the nature of his apologetic method. Though it is another extensive quote, it is worth reproducing it more or less in full as its content is vital for grasping the nature of Irenaeus' conception of apologetic method:

---

[85] As a methodological consideration, this same procedure of careful examination is found to varying degrees in many Patristic apologetic texts, from Origen's *Contra Celsum* to Athanasius' *Letters to Serapion on the Holy Spirit* to Gregory of Nyssa's *Contra Eunomium*.
[86] *AH*, XXXI.4.

In the first book... exposing (*arguentes*) 'knowledge falsely so called,' I showed (*ostendimus*) you... that the whole (*omne*) system devised... by those who are of the school of Valentinus, was false (*falsiloquium*) and baseless (*adinventum*). I also set forth the tenets (*sententias exposuimus*) of their predecessors, proving (*ostendentes*) that they not only differed (*discrepantes*) among themselves, but had long previously swerved from the truth itself. I further explained, with all diligence (*omni diligentia exposuimus*), the doctrine (*sententiam*) as well as practice (*operibus*) of Marcus the magician... and I carefully noticed (*diligenter retulimus*) the passages which they garble from the Scriptures, with the view of adapting them to their own fictions. Moreover, I minutely (*minutatim*) narrated[87] the manner in which (*quonam modo*), by means of numbers, and by the twenty-four letters of the alphabet, they boldly endeavour to establish [what they regard as] truth. I have also related how they think and teach... and what they hold... I mentioned (*diximus*), too, the multitude of those Gnostics who are sprung from him [Simon Magus], and noticed the points of difference (*differentia*)

---

[87] Carrying a sense consistent with Irenaeus, the Ante-Nicene Fathers volume containing the works of Irenaeus offers this Greek note for the underlying Latin of *perexivimus*: διεξήλθομεν, which the online Perseus Greek Word Study Tool link to Middle Liddell defines as: "to go through, pass through; to go through, go completely through; to go through in succession; to go through in detail, recount in full." See:
<http://www.perseus.tufts.edu/hopper/morph?l=diech%2Flqomen&la=greek&can=diech%2Flqomeno&prior=tau=ta#lexicon>, April 25, 2015.

between them, their several doctrines (*doctrinas*), and the order of their succession, while I set forth all (*omnes exposuimus*) those heresies which have been originated by them. I showed (*ostendimus*), moreover, that all these heretics, taking their rise from Simon, have introduced impious and irreligious doctrines (*dogmata*) into this life; and I explained (*manifestavimus*) the nature of their 'redemption,' and their method (*quomodo*) of initiating those who are rendered 'perfect,' along with their invocations and their mysteries. I proved also that there is one God, the Creator, and that He is not the fruit of any defect, nor is there anything either above Him, or after Him. In the present book, I shall establish those points which fit in with my design, so far as time permits, and overthrow (*evertimus*), by means of lengthened treatment under distinct heads, their whole system (*omnem ipsorum regulam*); for which reason, since it is an exposure (*detectio*) and subversion (*eversio*) of their opinions (*sententiae*), I have so entitled the composition of this work. For it is fitting (*oportet*), by a plain revelation (*indicium*) and overthrow (*eversionem*) of their conjunctions (*conjugationum*), to put an end (*dissolvere*) to these hidden alliances (*absconditas ipsorum conjugationes*), and to Bythus himself, and thus to obtain a demonstration (*ostensionem*) that he never existed at any previous time, nor now has any existence.[88]

---

[88] *AH*, II, pref. 1-2.

Irenaeus and Orthodox Apologetic Methodology

Key features of the above are numerous. For one, Irenaeus is consistently committed to the notion of detecting (*detectio*), of exposure (*arguentes*), of explaining (*manifestavimus*), and of showing, proving, and demonstrating (*ostendimus*) and setting forth all (*omnes exposuimus*) of how they are false (*falsiloquium*), innovationist (*adinventum*), and inconsistent (*discrepantes, differentia*) both among themselves and within their teachings. By exposing and showing their whole system (*omnem ipsorum regulam*) as false, he is able to overturn (*evertimus*) the danger fully and also to give others access so that they too can overturn it, can deconstruct and destroy (*dissolvere*) it fully. Again, he is committed to total exposure (*omnes exposuimus*), exposure of all (*omne*) of their doctrines and teachings (*doctrinas, dogmata*), their ways of thinking (*sententias*), and their ways and methods (*modo, quomodo*). Again, he also intends to be methodologically precise, exposing them with all diligence (*omni diligentia exposuimus*), scrupulously reporting (*diligenter retulimus*) their errors with systematically minute (*minutatim*) precision, including both their doctrine and their practice (*operibus*). In short, linked closely with his motive, Irenaeus' systematic methodology is one which treats the enemy doctrine as though it were the doctrinal equivalent of a ferocious brute that destroys multitudes (*multos vastantis*), a destructive beast (*bestiam*) that must be wounded (*vulnerare*) and killed (*interficere*) from all sides (*undique*).

Immediately following the Preface of Book II, Irenaeus again intimates his concern with being systematic, this time in the positive and constructive sense (rather than the purely deconstructive), by beginning the building of his case for orthodoxy *contra* error "with the first and most important head (*a primo et maximo capitulo*), that is, God the Creator."[89] As shown above, this is the same first principle of demonstration as found in his *Demonstration of the Apostolic Preaching*. Here, however, it emerges in the context of a key methodological distinction, for Irenaeus distinguishes between that of direct deconstruction, which is to say disproving them by considering them more or less purely on their own grounds, *secundum suam regulam*,[90] which he undertook in Book I, and that of construction *contra* error, which is to say overturning them by dialectically opposing it with an alternative. In this step of his methodology, their error is considered in dialectical tension with the truth as held by the Church - that of the "one and the same (*uno et eodem*) Being, the God and Father of all (*Patre omnia*), and not many diverse or derivative beings (*non alium atque alium, neque ex diversis diis aut virtutibus substantiam habentem*)."[91] As Book II's argument concludes and is, according to Irenaeus,[92] sufficiently proved (*sufficienter ostensa*), concerned as it is thematically with establishing (*ostenso*) "God alone, the Father" (*solo Deo Patre*) as the foundation for truth, Irenaeus also gives another important clue to his methodology:

> But that I may not be thought to avoid (*putemur fugere*) that series of proofs (*probationem*) which may be derived

---

[89] *AH*, II.1. Though there is not space to enter into this here, it seems that, at least as regards demonstration (*ostendere*) of the truth, rather than beginning with the cross, Irenaeus begins with God, the only Father (*solus Pater*).

[90] *AH*, II.XXXV.1.

[91] *AH*, II.XXXV.4.

[92] *arbitror quidem sufficienter ostensa, et per haec tanta uno ostenso Deo Patre factore omnium*

> from the Scriptures of the Lord (since, indeed, these Scriptures do much more evidently and clearly proclaim this very point), I shall, for the benefit of those at least who do not bring a depraved mind to bear upon them, devote a special book to the Scriptures referred to, which shall fairly follow them out [and explain them], and I shall plainly set forth from these divine Scriptures proofs to [satisfy] all the lovers of truth.[93]

Thus Irenaeus not only expresses his foundational conviction that the Scriptures are a basis for deriving proofs, *multo manifestius et clarius hoc ipsum praedicantibus*, which is itself a key component of his methodology, he also expresses a concern not to avoid (*putemur fugere*) making these Scriptural proofs. In other words, his commitment to thoroughness motivates and informs his apologetic methodology. Apologetics, according to Irenaeus, is thus systematic in both senses of the term, which is to say holistic in theory and methodical in practice, as is evident also from the size and nature of the work considered as a whole. Considering moreover that his intention is also pedagogical, that others also take up and expand upon this apologetic task,

---

[93] *AH*, II.XXXV.4. *Sed ne putemur fugere illam quae ex Scripturis Dominicis est probationem, ipsis Scripturis multo manifestius et clarius hoc ipsum praedicantibus, his tamen qui non prave intendunt, eis proprium librum, qui sequitur has Scripturas, reddentes, ex Scipturis divinis probationes apponemus in medio omnibus amantibus veritatem.*

his vision of apologetics implies that it also *ought* to be systematic in its theory and practice in the Church.[94]

Book III

That the preceding is not accidental, the opening of Book III succinctly sums up Irenaeus' methodology thus far. This includes reasserting his intention to demolish (*destruentem*) and contradict (*contradicere*) their ways of thinking (*sententias*); also to manifest (*manifestare*), show (*arguentes*), clearly reveal (*manifestum proderem*), and lay "bare and open to view" (*nudata et ostensa*) that which they would conceal (*absconditas*); moreover, not just against one but to "set forth arguments against them all" (*et omnibus eis contradicere*) in order that together they are "cast down and overthrown" (*destructa et eversa*).[95] He also sums up each book's main apologetic focus, intimating further the integral nature of the whole work, "taking these in connection with them," and establishing that the third book will be proofs adduced from Scripture.[96] In this third book, moreover, he emphasizes that his intention is that his audience receive from him "the means of combating and vanquishing (*arguendum et evertendum*) those who, in whatever manner (*quolibet modo male*), are propagating (*docent*) falsehood."[97]

More than systematic in the practical, methodical sense, Irenaeus' methodology is also "systems-atic," which is to

---

[94] The conclusion of Book II does not appear to add significantly to the present study, so its discussion is omitted.
[95] *AH*, III, pref.
[96] *AH*, III, pref.
[97] *AH*, III, pref.

Irenaeus and Orthodox Apologetic Methodology

say it is a "systems approach" that not only equips the Church with the means to thoroughly defeat the particulars of error, but does so via an apperception of the *regulam* of the heretics' *sententias*, their *modos* in whatever form it may take. By conceiving of error in this way, as a false system and not just a false conclusion, Irenaeus exposes most fully that his methodology is one of addressing the principle and impetus of error which is responsible for whatever form the error may take. Moreover, this section is also where Irenaeus instructs his audience that upon receiving and assimilating his "copious refutation of all the heretics" they are to "faithfully and strenuously (*fiducialiter ac instantissime*)… resist (*resistes*) them in defence of the only true and life-giving faith." In other words, according to Irenaeus the Church cannot be neutral.[98] There is no neutral common ground with heresy, and as such the Church is obligated to take a faithful stand against the heretical systems, to strenuously oppose their machinations. It must, moreover, critically identify and study the principles and means by which they operate and produce various falsehoods so that they can be exposed and overthrown.

At the end of Book III, Irenaeus makes a compassionate turn towards a more express pity. He states: "We do indeed pray that these men may not remain in the pit which they themselves

---

[98] This position, put forward by Irenaeus, provides for Orthodoxy a formidable obstacle to maintaining a myth of religious neutrality in regards to any non-Christian metaphysical scheme. For an extensive discussion of this phenomenon, not with an eye towards Patristic or Ancient philosophy but to Modern, see: Roy Clouser, *The Myth of Religious Neutrality: An essay on the Hidden Role of Religious Belief in Theories*, (Notre Dame, IN: University of Notre Dame Press, 2005).

have dug, but separate themselves... that they, being converted to the Church of God, may be lawfully begotten, and that Christ may be formed in them, and that they may know... the only true God."[99] Thus the destruction of their error is, in a manner of speaking, surgical, and born of love: "It may be compared to a severe remedy, extirpating the proud and sloughing flesh of a wound; for it puts an end to their pride and haughtiness."[100] This consideration places the severity of the methodology into a framework of healing which, although not mitigating the force of the refutation, yet keeps in mind their need of salvation. As Irenaeus states: "We pray for these things on their behalf, loving them better than they seem to love themselves. For our love, inasmuch as it is true, is salutary to them, if they will but receive it." Apologetics, thus, is in a sense a thankless task of cauterization, of weaponized effort towards disarmament, born of love and yet carried out with vigorous dialectical opposition.

Irenaeus thus addresses one of the perennial problems Christians face: the manner of disagreeing with someone while at the same time having a compassionate disposition towards them as persons. To love is not necessarily to agree, and to disagree, even vigorously, as Irenaeus shows, is not the same thing as hating.[101] Without this distinction apologetics is

---

[99] *AH*, III.XXV.7
[100] *AH*, III.XXV.7
[101] Though modern ears may be dismayed at the intensity of this form of polemic, it must however be understood according to its Christian presupposition. In a similar manner both John the Baptist and Christ each describe their opponents as a "brood of vipers." See Mat 3:7, 12:34, 23:33, and Luke 3:7.

impossible, or must necessarily end in either emotional aggression or physical violence. The fact that Irenaeus, as an historiographic observation of the Ante-Nicene Church, was in no position to generate institutional "force," but instead relied on reasoned appeal, shows that vigorous apologetics is possible. Thus this hatred of error was vigorous, and the advocacy of truth relentless, but at the same time a sense of compassion for those in error remained an abiding presence.

      This sense of compassion, rather than attenuating the motive to overthrow, actually functions to reinforce and even increase the intensity of effort: "Wherefore it shall not weary us, to endeavor with all our might to stretch out the hand to them."[102] Love thus serves as an endless source of inspiration to renew the apologetic effort. Without first overthrowing their false doctrine, however, those in error are yet in need to "stand away from the void, and relinquish the shadow," which assists in explaining why Irenaeus, "over and above what has already been stated," has "deferred to the following book, to adduce the words of the Lord; if, by convincing some among them, through means of the very instruction of Christ," he "may succeed in persuading them to abandon such error, and to cease from blaspheming their Creator."[103] In other words, only after three long and painstaking books focused on overthrowal does Irenaeus begin to speak in more explicit tones of persuasion. This has deep ramifications for understanding the nature of Irenaeus' vision of the apologetic effort. The first, and lengthier, stage is composed itself of three distinct steps, that of first

---

[102] *AH*, III.XXV.7
[103] *AH*, III.XXV.7

exposing and deconstructing the heresy on its own grounds, the second step being the exposure and deconstruction of the heresy on the grounds of an alternative which is more true,[104] and the third step to deconstruct and overthrow according to direct reference to Scriptural proof.[105] Only after all this has been painstakingly completed is a more forthright consideration of persuasion broached. In reference to this hope for persuasion and conversion, it is also worth noting that this is the only book which ends with a prayer followed by an Amen.[106]

Book IV

---

[104] This second step is also characterized by a focus on God the Father, the foundation and first principle from which Irenaeus builds his system of constructive demonstration, as also in his *Demonstration of the Apostolic Preaching*, a fact which indicates it is neither accidental nor merely restricted to arguments against pseudo-gnostics, but is actually integral to Irenaeus' thought.

[105] Of course, much of the deconstruction and overthrowal is in the form of defeating them by implicating them in self-refutation.

[106] The notion of persuasion and conversion which Irenaeus takes up as a methodological principle only *after* heresy has been overthrown also implies that there is perhaps a functional distinction between apologetics and "evangelism." Taking the passage from 1 Peter 3:15 as a reference, if apologetics is the *defense* of the hope of salvation, then evangelism is the communication of this hope. Evangelism may be inseparable from apologetics in the broad context of Christian life and theology, and their distinguishing edges may be somewhat blurred, but the two also ought not be confused, either. Evangelism *qua* evangelism does not intrinsically imply either defense or embattlement, whereas apologetics does. To evangelize is to declare the Good News, whereas apologetics is the defense of this Good News. Of course, evangelism can transition and become apologetic, and vice versa, but the point remains that according to their essential functions they are better understood as distinct activities.

Irenaeus and Orthodox Apologetic Methodology

Book IV begins a second and more explicitly persuasive stage, preceded by the first which was in three steps, as discussed above. This second stage Irenaeus reportedly intends so that his audience "turning them [the heretics] into the haven of the truth, mayest cause them to attain their salvation."[107] In the opening phrases he expresses that this book is to "add weight" to what he has already advanced so that, having "the means of confuting (*confutandos*) all the heretics everywhere," the faithful might further "not permit them... to launch out further into the deep of error, nor to be drowned in the sea of ignorance."[108] The prior detection and refutation of their error, then, prosecuted with such diligence, is now used to stop their further advance, "beaten back at all points" (*omnimodo retusos*), so that they do not further court their own destruction.

    This process of refutation followed by persuasion unto conversion (*convertere*), however, is by no means a matter of mere rhetorical flourish. It is, according to Irenaeus, the application of a careful and thorough knowledge, like unto that which he has laboriously imparted, wherein the person "must possess an accurate knowledge (*diligenter scire*) of their systems or schemes of doctrine (*regulas sive argumenta ipsorum*)." It is in this context where Irenaeus again makes reference to the healing of a disease: "For it is impossible for anyone to heal (*curare*) the sick (*male habentes*), if he has no knowledge (*ignorat*) of the disease (*passionem*) of the patients (*male valent*)."[109] In

---

[107] *AH*, pref. IV.1.

[108] *AH*, pref. IV.1. *non longius sinas erroris procedere profundum, neque ignorantiae praefocari pelago*

[109] *AH*, pref. IV.2.

order to heal the heretics of their error, then, one must be trained, deeply knowledgeable of the afflicting disease. It is ignorance of this heretical system (*quia ignorabant regulam ipsorum*), the heretical system which Irenaeus has "with all care (*omni diligentia*) delivered," that Irenaeus attributes the inability of his predecessors to refute (*contradicere*), in particular, the Valentinians.[110] Though not apparently forbidden in principle to anyone among the faithful, clearly apologetics is an advanced discipline.

It is also in this same section where Irenaeus makes another "systematics move" when he asserts of the first book's exposition that the Valentinian "doctrine is a recapitulation of all the heretics."[111] This is especially significant because it intimates that there is a universal dimension intended by Irenaeus for his text. Therefore, once the Valentinians are refuted, because they recapitulate a yet more archetypal principle and system of heresy, the text itself can still stand as a model by which to learn how to "overthrow every kind of heresy."[112] This is possible, according to Irenaeus, because "they who oppose these men by the right method (*secundum quod oportet*), do [thereby] oppose all who are of an evil mind."[113] In this light, then, it is clear that Irenaeus is thinking in terms of whole systems, and as a consequence it is arguable that his

---

[110] *AH*, pref. IV.2.

[111] *in quo et ostendimus doctrinam eorum recapitulationem esse omnium haereticorum*

[112] *AH*, pref. IV.2. *evertunt omnem haeresim*

[113] *AH*, pref. IV.2. *qui enim his contradicunt secundum quod oportet, contradicunt omnibus qui sunt malae sententiae*

attention to detail is coterminous with his sense for pattern, for *regula*. It is the root of the system that is blasphemous.[114] By discerning the *regula* on which the error is based and produced, then, one can provide for its and all heresies' "entire discomfiture" (*totius eversionis*).[115]

Irenaeus is not silent concerning that which unifies the heretics:

> For all these, although they issue forth from diverse regions, and promulgate different [opinions], do nevertheless concur in the same blasphemous design (*blasphemiae concurrunt propositum*), wounding [men] unto death, by teaching blasphemy against God our Maker and Supporter, and derogating from the salvation of man.[116]

The two primary themes are that of blasphemy against God and obviating man's salvation.[117] The heretics are even understood by Irenaeus to be the means of the "apostate angel" (*apostata angelus*) to effect the disobedience of mankind.[118] The heretics are in a grave sense participating in a much more primal struggle than merely that of various or competing schools of thought: "This, then, is the aim of him who envies our life, to

---

[114] *AH*, pref. IV.3. *super omnes est enim blasphema regula ipsorum*

[115] *AH*, pref. IV.2.

[116] *AH*, pref. IV.4.

[117] A little further down Irenaeus reasserts these same two as the constant of the heretics: "For whatsoever all the heretics may have advanced with the utmost solemnity, they come to this at last, that they blaspheme the Creator, and disallow the salvation of God's workmanship, which the flesh truly is."

[118] *AH*, pref. IV.4.

render men disbelievers in their own salvation, and blasphemous against God the Creator." Apologetics thus for Irenaeus has an intrinsic connection with the "whole dispensation" (*omnem dispositionem*) of the Son of God, for "which [he] proved, in a variety of ways" (*multis modis ostendimus*) against the blasphemous *regula* of the heretics.[119]

Moreover, though it could seem simplistic to refer the heretics' impetus back to the apostate angel, a couple features of Irenaeus apologetic mitigate this seeming. For one, this argument is set precisely in a context wherein Irenaeus is most intent on communicating a sense of compassionate responsibility for heretics, desiring not simply to destroy them as persons, but to destroy the illness they are infected with and so to heal that which is wounded. Secondly, Irenaeus' argument does not collapse into mere strutting. He has invested enormous resources to argue carefully, thoroughly, and diligently, and thus his appeal to the envious one is not a retreat into bigoted ignorance, but the declaration of an integrated spiritual, if not cosmic, dimension to human activity. The entire physical and spiritual reality is implicated in Irenaeus' apologetic theology, and as such his appeal to "him who envies our life" is actually an expression of theological coherence and consistency.[120] Needless to say, this increases both the scope and the gravity of Irenaeus' conception of apologetics.

The end of Book IV continues the above theme about the relationship heretics have with the devil, as their chief

---

[119] *AH*, pref. IV.4.
[120] *AH*, pref. IV.4.

Irenaeus and Orthodox Apologetic Methodology

(*diabolo adscribuntur principi*).[121] It is, however, this very factor which further motivates Irenaeus' apologetic: "It was incumbent also upon me, for their own sake,[122] to refute by many [arguments] (*per multa confutare*) those who are involved in many errors,[123] if by any means, when they are confuted by many [proofs], they may be converted to the truth and saved."[124] It is precisely this effort for their sake which causes Irenaeus to argue with such vigorous length and detail, to show that their error has no ground, that it is false and baseless. Thus refutation and confutation, albeit methodologically thorough and in this sense severe, are also rendered surgical tools for healing those who might be converted to the truth and thus saved. Utterly removing his apologetic from mere intellectualism, the type of error Irenaeus is battling has profound spiritual consequences, and so his apologetic methodology, in all its careful and massive output, is very much motivated by this transcendental, compassionate concern.

In light of the foregoing, the Scriptures and their interpretation become a type of battleground. This naturally also informs his apologetic methodology, and is one of the reported reasons for his fifth and final book dealing with the "complete (*integrum*) exposure and refutation (*contradictionem*) of knowledge, falsely so-called."[125] Irenaeus states that it is

---

[121] *AH*, IV.XLI.3.
[122] *oportebat et nos propter eos*
[123] *qui in multis erroribus continentur*
[124] *AH*, IV.XLI.4. *si quo modo possent per multa confutati ad veritatem converti et salvari*
[125] *AH*, IV.XLI.4.

necessary to add to this pedagogical and systematic preparation for apologetics the fifth and final book so as "to explain whatsoever [Scriptural passages] have received other interpretations from the heretics, who have altogether misunderstood what Paul has spoken, and to point out the folly of their mad (*dementiam*) opinions."[126] Apologetically oriented exposition of Scripture, then, functions within the systematic methodology which he is supplying or furnishing (*praebebimus*) his audience. This, then, completes the means by which they can most effectively oppose, overthrow, disgrace (*exprobrationis*), and destroy whole false systems, refuting "all heretics" (omnium haereticorum).[127]

Book V
The fifth and final book has a short preface, but it supplies yet further key elements motivating and informing the ordering of Irenaeus' systematic apologetic methodology.[128] First he summarizes the intentions of the previous four books, that of firstly exposing all the heretics, bringing their erroneous doctrines to light, and refuting those who have "devised irreligious opinions" (*irreligiosas adinvenerunt sententias*).[129] Then he makes a key distinction between, on the one hand, making arguments particularly suited to particular false doctrines (*ex propria uniuscujusque illorum doctrina*), and, on the other hand, making arguments "of a more general nature, and applicable to

---

[126] *AH*, IV.XLI.4.
[127] *AH*, IV.XLI.4.
[128] A conclusion to the work has apparently not survived.
[129] *AH*, V, pref.

them all" (*ex ratione universis ostensionibus procedente*). This distinction is vital for enabling both the tailoring of arguments to suit specific heresies as well as recognizing common patterns of error applicable to all. It is this distinction, moreover, which, transcending pure Patristics, makes an Irenaean understanding of systematic apologetic methodology possible, and grounds his apologetics in the field of systematic theology together with his strategies of critical exposure and analysis, rational argumentation, logical demonstration from first principles, and global deconstruction, all grounded in and presupposing Scriptural and Apostolic authority in a cosmic Christian worldview.

    The next stage is where Irenaeus asserts how he has conceived his efforts thus far, that he "pointed out the truth, and shown the preaching of the Church."[130] In Book II this was seen to be generally founded on the first principle of Irenaeus' method of demonstration, that of God's necessary existence and supreme oneness. Irenaeus developed this in Book III based on Scriptural teaching, as received by the Church, after which, in another stage, he "disposed of all questions which the heretics proposed to us." This is followed by an exposition of the doctrine of the apostles and the parables of the Lord, and then, finally, completed in the fifth and final book by exhibiting "proofs from the rest of the Lord's doctrine and the apostolical epistles."[131] To enumerate these, there would seem to be eight distinct aspects to what Irenaeus conceives in the fifth book as constituting his apologetic efforts:

---

[130] *AH*, V, Preface.
[131] *AH*, V, Preface.

1. Particular arguments - via setting forth their particular opinions.
2. General arguments - via a treatment of their doctrines' consequences and basic principles of reason.[132]
3. Pointing out the truth - largely an argument from reason, either indirectly as an antithesis to their absurdity, or directly by reference to Scripture.[133]
4. Showing the Church's preaching - arguments from Scripture.
5. Disposing of heretic's proposed questions.
6. Explaining Apostolic doctrine.
7. Setting forth the import of the Lord's parables.
8. Exhibiting proofs from the rest of the Lord's doctrine and the apostolical epistles.

To reiterate, it is not precisely the intention of the present study to ascertain definitively whether or not Irenaeus was entirely successful in any of his arguments or whether he was interested in implementing the above strategy such that, say, each book corresponds distinctly and indubitably to each one or two of the aspects listed above or, moreover, that elements of the above list do not overlap or bleed into each other. The list seems to be Irenaeus' own self-conception of his efforts. Nor is it of present interest to determine how or in what

---

[132] The constant appeals to rational argumentation, inconsistency on the part of the heretics, their falling into madness, etc., is ample proof of Irenaeus' commitment to reason in his practice of apologetics.

[133] Cf. *AH*, II.XXVIII.1: "Having therefore the truth itself as our rule..."

Irenaeus and Orthodox Apologetic Methodology

ways Irenaeus, in a practical sense, either distinguishes or fuses the elements of the above list into the particular sections of his larger work. The present, primary concern, that of systematic theology, is that of the nature and scope of the proposed system, not how closely its architect follows or fails to follow his own prescription. It also does not assert that the above list exhausts all the key elements of his methodology, such as his metaphysical, epistemological, ethical, and ecclesial (etc.) concerns. Of course, Irenaeus is largely faithful to his own scheme, even if it is debatable to what extent the eight aspects listed above relate, overlap, or interpenetrate, or whether or not they fall distinctly into one or another of his five books. To be sure, he gives other summaries of each book's efforts, to varying degrees, at the beginning and end of each one, yet, this final one, not so much concerned with articulating to which book belongs which aspect, abstracts the aspects in a way especially suited to systematic treatment, moreover demonstrating Irenaeus' consistently systematic mind.

That said, the above schema illustrates positively how Irenaeus conceives of the various elements of a successful apologetic system. Held in the light of his painstaking, meticulous, and lengthy effort to utterly expose the heretics and their doctrines, to refute, overthrow, and destroy their entire system, and moreover to hold out a hope that, after all this, cured of their madness, they might turn away from their blasphemy of God and away from their denial of salvation, Irenaeus thus demonstrates a fairly comprehensive model of what apologetics is, both as regards its motives and its methods.

Irenaeus and Orthodox Apologetic Methodology

Before concluding with this running exposition of Irenaeus' motives and methodology, Book V offers yet two more key elements. After reiterating that he labored "by every means in [his] power to furnish thee with large assistance against the contradictions of the heretics, as also to reclaim the wanderers and convert them to the Church," Irenaeus adds another element, that his systematic apologetics functions:

> to confirm at the same time the minds of the neophytes, that they may preserve stedfast the faith which they received, guarded by the Church in its integrity, in order that they be in no way perverted by those who endeavor to teach them false doctrines, and lead them away from the truth.[134]

In other words, the extended, analytical deconstruction and systematic overthrowal of untruth as worked out over five books plays a role according to Irenaeus, in stabilizing those neophytes who are first appropriating the faith. Apologetics is thus not intended to be sequestered among the intellectual aristocracy, but is proper to the faithful as a catholic inheritance, appropriate for raising up stable, faithful Christians who are strengthened to preserve the faith they have received, with minds confirmed via apologetics such that they are enabled to consciously counter false doctrines which could otherwise lead them unawares from the truth. This has far reaching implications, for it shows not only that there is a

---

[134] *AH*, V. pref. *neophytorum quoque sensum confirmare, ut stabilem custodiant fidem, quam bene custoditam ab Ecclesia acceperunt, ut nullo modo transvertantur ab his, qui male docere eos, et abducere a veritate conantur.*

critical intellectual component to the apostolic faith as understood by Irenaeus, but that apologetics ought to pervade the life of this intellectually defensible faith, being useful for stabilizing beginners.

The second key element follows upon this one, and is especially vital as it concerns and confirms the apparently universal scope Irenaeus envisions for his work, which is to say, its normative applicability:

> It will be incumbent (*oportebit*) upon you, however, and all (*omnesque*) who may happen to read this writing, to peruse with great attention (*impensius legere*) what I have already said, that you may obtain a knowledge (*scias*) of the subjects against which I am contending. For it is thus that you will both controvert them in a legitimate manner (*legitime eis contradices*), and will be prepared to receive (*praeparato accipies*) the proofs brought forward against them, casting away their doctrines as filth by means of the celestial faith; but following the only true and steadfast Teacher, the Word of God, our Lord Jesus Christ, who did, through His transcendent love, become what we are, that He might bring us to be even what He is Himself.[135]

---

[135] *AH*, V. pref. *Oportebit autem te, omnesque lecturos hanc scripturam, impensius legere ea quae a nobis praedicta sunt, ut et argumenta ipsa scias, adversus quae contradictiones facimus. Sic enim et legitime eis contradices, et de praeparato accipies adversus eos contradictiones, illorum quidem sententias per coelestem fidem, velut stercora, abjiciens; solum autem verum et firmum magistrum sequens, Verbum Dei, Jesum Christum Dominum nostrum: qui propter immensam suam dilectionem factus est quod sumus nos, uti nos perficeret esse quod et ipse.*

Thus Irenaeus sees his effort as necessary (*oportebit*) for legitimately (*legitime*) opposing the enemies of the truth of the apostolic faith. This shows moreover that there is a legitimate as well as an illegitimate, or improper, method of apologetics in Irenaeus' mind, which as shown above was the reason he proffered as to why his predecessors had not been able to subvert the heretics, for they had not followed the proper method of close, full-orbed analytical method as modelled (only later, of course) by Irenaeus. He expresses, moreover, that all (*omnesque*) those who read his work ought to do so with great care in order to effect the purposes intended for the work as a whole. Again the universal scope and intention of the work is affirmed. Though, historically, not all were literate, the point is clear that Irenaeus is not giving any express limit as to who has permission to learn and apply his method for both their own stability and the stability of others. By closely attending to both his arguments and his methods, the faithful reader will be prepared to do apologetics successfully.

ASSESSMENT IN LIGHT OF CONTEMPORARY APOLOGETIC DISCOURSE

The foregoing analysis would seem to indicate that Irenaeus has a clear sense of the proper way to refute arguments and account for the faith, i.e. a proper way to do apologetics. In other words, according to him there is a legitimate apologetic methodology. Recalling, then, the definitions of apologetics given above, Irenaeus' work is clearly apologetic in nature and scope, and moreover seems especially to correspond to some degree with Frame's notion of "offensive apologetics," a method common to all forms of Presuppositional Apologetic methodology, which is to say that of whole-system destruction. For example, as Bahnsen observes of Van Til's methodology: "entire systems are in opposition."[136] As Florovsky points out: "The truth was, according to St. Irenaeus, a 'well-grounded system,' a *corpus* (*adv. haeres*. II. 27. 1 — *veritatis corpus*), a '*harmonious melody*' (II. 38. 3)."[137] Christianity, being in this sense a system, not only is Irenaean apologetic methodology defensive, answering specific questions and objections raised by heretics, not only does it offer constructive demonstration and proof of the fundamentals of the Christian system, but it is also offensive insofar as it seeks, as a true system, to put the whole of a false system into view so as to destroy it *in toto*, as one whole in opposition to another whole.

Further justifying the above Irenaean notion of system, Hefner states in his article on Irenaeus' theological methodology: "The one highest authority for Irenaeus is the system, framework, or 'hypothesis' of the faith."[138] Though this argument is articulated in reference to Irenaeus' theological system, it bears close and supportive resemblance to the findings of the present study concerning specifically Irenaeus' apologetic methodology. In a sense it is only natural that

---

[136] *Van Til's Apologetic*, 268.

[137] Georges Florovsky, *Bible, Church, Tradition: An Eastern Orthodox View*, (Belmont, MA: Nordland Publishing, 1972), 79.

[138] Philip Hefner, "Theological Methodology and St. Irenaeus," The Journal of Religion, Vol. 44, No. 4 (Oct., 1964), pp. 294-309, 295.

Irenaeus' apologetics would correspond with his larger theological methodology. Of his *Adversus Haereses* Hefner continues: "Irenaeus' total theological enterprise in the *Adversus haereses* is to establish the hegemony of this 'hypothesis' over and against another 'hypothesis' which the heretics have put forth."[139] The very text stands in this light as the systematic manifestation of its own hypothesis, apologetically exercising the principle insight into the intrinsic relationship between a hypothesis and its manifestation in terms of a system; in this case one hypothesis opposing another in terms of their mutually elaborated systems.

The term "system," however, is liable to equivocation and therefore confusion in that, arguing for or against even the very notion of system in theology, one applies a single aspect of the term in cases where the other ought to be applied. For example, one easy misunderstanding is that, in order to qualify as a system or even as a work of "systematics," a work must be linearly methodical or symmetrically programmatic, i.e. "orderly."[140] Rather, systematics is, or is at least functioning in

---

[139] Hefner, 295-6. See below for a more extended discussion of the notion of *hypothesis*.

[140] Reflecting this possibility for equivocation, the American Heritage Dictionary gives two definitions of systematic: "1. Characterized by, based on, or constituting a system: systematic thought. 2. Working or done in a step-by-step manner; methodical: a systematic worker; a systematic approach." In the first definition, there is nothing necessitating that it be "step-by-step," but merely that it "based on" a system. The second definition, however, refers directly to methodical, step-by-step procedure. In criticizing "systematic theology," there is a tendency to take the meaning given in the second definition as representing the essence of that which is systematic when, however, the first definition is not necessarily implicated in the second. As such, it is entirely possible to "do systematics" without being rigidly bound to

the present study as referring to, in essence, coherence. The term systematic itself comes from the Greek συστηματικός, which has been defined as meaning "of or like an organized whole."[141] In the present context, then, a "system" can be understood as that wherein elements cohere, at least in "intention," such that what is at the end aligns holistically with what is at the beginning and also with what is in the middle. The *content* of a text can therefore be described as "systematic" insofar as its elements cohere relative to the whole, even if the manifest *structure* of the text is not systematic. It does not have to "appear" ordered or even orderly, as "organization" can take many forms, though of course in practice systematics does generally tend in this direction, hence the mistaking of one expression of systematics for the whole. In short, not "order in

---

step-by-step schematic or procedural considerations. See *American Heritage® Dictionary of the English Language*, Fifth Edition. S.v. "systematic." <http://www.thefreedictionary.com/systematic>, April 25, 2015.

    Wayne Grudem, in his massive work on the subject, offers this definition of *systematic theology*, which he distinguishes from apologetics: "Systematic theology is any study that answers the question, 'What does the whole Bible teach us today?' about any given topic" (Wayne Grudem, *Systematic Theology*, (Grand Rapids, MI: Zondervan, jointly with IVP, 1994), 21). This definition also does not necessitate rigid, step-by-step procedure.

    For a discussion of the various ways in which systematic theology is understood, see Michael Williams' essay, "Systematic Theology as a Biblical Discipline," in *All for Jesus: A Celebration of the 50th Anniversary of Covenant Theological Seminary*, eds. R.A. Paterson and S.M. Lucas, (Fearn, Ross Shire: Christian Focus, 2005), 197-233.

[141] Henry George Liddell and Robert Scott, *A Greek-English Lexicon*, rev. and aug. Sir Henry Stuart Jones with Roderick McKenzie, (Oxford: Clarendon Press, 1940).

theology," systematic theology is "coherence in theology."[142] Basically, a work qualifies as essentially or intrinsically systematic if throughout its discourse it maintains a constant position, say, of epistemological realism, and consistent, unequivocal use of terms, say, where the term Jesus Christ always refers to He who is fully God and fully man in the Chalcedonian sense, etc. On the other hand, a work is unsystematic if the end does not cohere with the beginning or the middle, and if the terms are used equivocally - even if the structure has the appearance of system. This is not to say a work must contain zero errata in order to qualify as systematic, or be undebatable in the positions it takes. Whether or not a work is explicitly ordered according to a readily identifiable programme, however, is not the fundamental criteria for determining whether or not it is systematic, but rather its pervasive coherence.

In seeming correspondence with Hefner, Florovsky also states: "Christian dogmatics itself is the only true philosophical 'system.'"[143] In other words, recalling the definition of apologetics coming from the *Dictionary of Scholastic Philosophy*, with connections to Andreyev's notion of apologetics, Christianity understood as a system provides a comprehensive view of the world, or worldview, by speaking comprehensively

---

[142] It is important to keep in mind the distinction between "*a*" systematic theology, which is to say a particular expression of systematic theology, including its particular modes of organization, with systematic theology as a general notion, unrelated in its essence to any particular organizational scheme.

[143] Georges Florovsky, *Creation and Redemption*, (Belmont, MA: Nordland Publishing, 1976), 33.

and authoritatively to the fundamental philosophical issues of metaphysics, epistemology, and ethics according to, in Irenaean terms, "'the rule of truth,' κανών της αληθείας, *régula veritatis*."[144] Gordon Clark, expressing a sentiment similar to Florovsky's, states: "Christianity is a comprehensive view of all things: it takes the world, both material and spiritual, to be an ordered system."[145]

This notion of worldview, therefore, can be observed to bear an immanent relationship with the notion of *regulam* understood as a system, as a rule for arranging and viewing not just one thing but all things together.[146] Of course, this touches on key epistemological considerations, an issue which recalls an important aspect of contemporary apologetic methodologies such as found in Reformed Epistemological and Presuppositional. In Book V.I.1, for example, Irenaeus makes a key epistemological claim: "For in no other way could we have learned the things of God, unless our Master, existing as the Word, had become man. For no other being had the power of revealing to us the things of the Father, except His own proper

---

[144] Florovsky, *Bible, Church, Tradition*, 78. Florovsky states elsewhere: "... *the truth of faith* is also the truth *for* reason and *for* thought - this does not mean, however, that it is the truth of thought, the truth of pure reason. The truth of faith is fact, reality—*that which is*" (Florovsky, *Creation and Redemption*, 30). The faith, and its canon, are canons *for* reasoning and canons *for* thought. In another telling phrase, Florovsky asserts: "Usually we do not sufficiently perceive the entire significance of this transformation which Christianity introduced into the realm of thought" (ibid, 33-4).

[145] Gordon Clark, *A Christian View of Men and Things: An Introduction to Philosophy*, (Grand Rapids, MI: Eerdmans, 1952), 25.

[146] Charlton T. Lewis, *An Elementary Latin Dictionary*, (New York, Cincinnati, and Chicago: American Book Company, 1890).

Irenaeus and Orthodox Apologetic Methodology

Word." Presuppositional apologist Greg Bahnsen called this approach to knowledge "revelational epistemology."[147] Bahnsen, though not making any reference to Irenaeus, in a particularly lucid paragraph states the problematic via two key questions:

> Now if the epistemic importance of a context applies to individual words and to simple assertions, we can ask where one acquires the broader context for paragraphs of thought, large-scale judgments, ultimate conclusions about "reality." How does one arrive at a system of universal interpretive principles that can relate particular thoughts of facts to one another? Within what context does one synthesize his knowledge into a coherent system?[148]

In answer to Bahnsen's first question, Irenaeus would likely refer to the *canon* of truth, for it is this *canon* which integrates the "tiles" into the proper "mosaic." In answer to Bahnsen's second question, the context is the "traditioning" Church, the apologetically-armed guardian of revelation's truth claims. In other words, it is Christian revelation as maintained according to the *canon* of truth which is the ground and provider of epistemic access to truth, for, in Irenaeus' language, "in no other way could we have learned the things of God." Bahnsen would then seem to be in agreement with Irenaeus on this epistemological point, for without the *canon* of truth,

---

[147] Greg Bahnsen, *Presuppositional Apologetics: Stated and Defended*, ed. Joel McDurmon, (Powder Springs: The American Vision. Nacogdoches: Covenant Media Press. 2011), 273-78.
[148] Bahnsen, *Presuppositional Apologetics*, 273.

without the *canon* of "universal interpretive principles," without a revelational epistemology, there is zero possibility of arriving at a system comprised of true knowledge. The epistemological question therefore asserts itself as revelational and within an Irenaean notion of *canon*, especially insofar as *canon* is immanent to system.

As Irenaeus consistently argues the Father as his First Principle, it is also evident that his apologetic methodology approaches the subject of Christ consequent to his arguments from the Father. As an epistemological consideration, however, Christ seems to function as an *epistemological* first principle. Thus it seems that the Father functions as Irenaeus' metaphysical or ontological first principle, the one on which his metaphysical system is established, whereas Christ as an epistemological first principle *reveals* that which is ontologically (though not chronologically) prior: "For in no other way could we have learned the things of God, unless our Master, existing as the Word, had become man. For no other being had the power of revealing to us the things of the Father, except His own proper Word."[149] Though there is not space to argue this

---

[149] *AH*, V.I.1. There is not space to explore the role Irenaeus conceives of the Holy Spirit in (existentially?) revealing Christ who, in turn, reveals the Father. For some indication of the epistemological considerations Irenaeus is dealing with, see also *Demonstration*, 1.5, 6, and especially 7. For an extended study of the Holy Spirit in Irenaeus, see: Anthony Briggman, *Irenaeus of Lyons and the Theology of the Holy Spirit*, (Oxford: Oxford University Press, 2012). It might also be said that the above considerations of Christ as an epistemological first principle is by no means a reduction or isolation of Christ to this issue alone, as if He plays no role in Irenaeus' metaphysics, ethics, etc. Clearly Irenaeus implicates both Christ and the Spirit in the very act of Creation itself; see Demonstration 1.5-6.

fully here, nor to integrate this with his doctrine of Scripture, it is however a fundamental operational principle for apologetics as Irenaeus practices it.[150] Even his appeal to Scripture comes posterior to his argument for the singular Creator, for it seems that Irenaeus intuits that apologetic methodology has a proper order such that after a critical deconstruction of the false on its own terms, Irenaeus then establishes the ontological and monarchic First Principle as a critical anti-gnostic counter-principle on which to establish his positive case for Christian orthodoxy. It is only after this that Irenaeus argues extensively from Scripture according to the rule of truth, the *canon* that is epistemologically revealed by Christ and traditioned by the Apostles to the Church. Both a practical and theoretical consideration, then, Irenaeus arrives at his epistemological first principle from his metaphysical first principle.[151]

---

[150] For Irenaeus' idea that the Church is the repository of truth: "Since therefore we have such proofs, it is not necessary to seek the truth among others which it is easy to obtain from the Church" (*AH*, III.IV.1). This also points towards a methodological principle for apologetics being especially grounded in the Church. Likewise, and touching also on the unity of the Church together with the Scriptures: "Since, therefore, the tradition from the apostles does thus exist in the Church, and is permanent among us, let us revert to the Scriptural proof" (*AH*, III.V.1). It might also be observed that Irenaeus precedes and justifies these arguments on grounds of historical argumentation, which not incidentally is a method of Evidential Apologetics. The Scriptures, which record the Gospel, are handed down in the Church. The Gospel, as set down in the Scriptures and maintained in the Church, the Gospel which Irenaeus describes as the "ground and pillar of our faith," is thus together with the Church is the *epistemological context* in which Christ, the epistemological first principle, is set forth in time and space. (See III.I.1)

[151] For example, as a practical methodological consideration in light of the above, according to Irenaeus it would make little sense to argue the subtleties of Christology without God as a metaphysical presupposition, for Christology

Irenaeus and Orthodox Apologetic Methodology

Two aspects of the same whole, it is the *canon* or *regulam* which causes the system, and the system which expresses or unfolds that which the *regulam* inherently or enfoldedly contains within itself.[152] Contextually, considering that Irenaeus is addressing the entire pseudo-gnostic system, *regulam* thus takes on a more pervasive scope, not as a mere abstract isolated rule, but as that which works to produce the false system from within, as in the equation which produces and is enfoldedly

---

would otherwise have no context. It could seem strange that Irenaeus leads the constructive portion of his argument with his metaphysical first principle rather than with his epistemological first principle, but since knowledge is always knowledge of some being or thing, the being in question is presupposed as logically prior (though not necessarily chronologically prior) to any knowledge of it. In this sense, knowledge, requisite in any act of knowing some being or thing, is in practice coterminous with metaphysics, for the epistemological first principle is *implicit* throughout the entirety of the metaphysical argument for God, but in Irenaeus' mind (at least as manifested in his text), when considered explicitly as an identifiable principle, his Christological principle of knowledge *as a first principle* of epistemology is made *explicit* only later. In his *Demonstration* it is clear, however, that prior to entering into the demonstration of the metaphysical first principle of God the Father, there is a lived context of (unphilosophically developed) Trinitarian baptismal entry into the faith. (See *Demonstration* 1.3) Faith, then, seems to be the existential condition in which the demonstration from metaphysical first principles proceeds.

[152] For a discussion of Irenaeus' notion of the *regula fidei*, see Paul Blowers, "The *Regula Fidei* and the Narrative Character of Early Christian Faith," Pro Ecclesia Vol. VI, No.2, 199-228. Blowers sets the canon or rule of faith in terms of a "narrative construction" that sets forth "'the dramatic' structure of a Christian vision of the world, posing as an hermeneutical frame of reference for the interpretation of Christian Scripture and Christian experience, and educing the first principles of Christian theological discourse and of a doctrinal substantiation of Christian faith" (Blowers, 202). Moreover, a "kind of framework" (Blowers, 210), he also connects in company with Rowan Williams this rule of faith with the establishing (and by extension defense) of Christian identity, an observation which places apologetics close to the core of the Christian experience. (Blowers, 203)

intrinsic to a fractal, or the genotype which produces, together with the particularities of environment, a phenotype. Irenaeus is thus not only systematic, but systems-atic, which is to say in apperceiving a *canon* (*regulam*, κανών) he treats a system *in toto*. In fact, without access to the inner logic, *hypothesis*, pattern, or *canon* of a system, it is impossible to determine with any certainty which mosaic image is correct.[153] Since it is the *canon* which produces the mosaic of elements, either according to a true or false *canon*, it is thus the *canon* which is intrinsically related to the whole system of mosaic tiles from within, as two aspects of the same whole. Each necessarily implying the other, *canon* is in this sense the primary engine of system and so of worldview, and worldview is likewise the necessary consequence of some *canon*.

Moreover, though the distinction has not been elaborated up to this point, there is an inextricable relationship between *hypothesis* and *canon*.[154] According to Behr's view, it seems that a *hypothesis* is a yet more inward facet of a *canon*. As Behr states, a canon is "an articulation of the hypothesis in a particular situation, outlining the presupposition needed for seeing..."[155] This description is slightly adjusted towards the more systematic as Behr quotes Clement's definitional use of *canon*: "The ecclesiastical canon is the concord and symphony of

---

[153] Florovsky also discusses Irenaeus' notion of *canon* and its relation to Irenaeus' mosaic analogy. See Florovsky, *Bible, Church, Tradition: An Eastern Orthodox View*, 77-79. For a listing and discussion of some of these key Greek and Latin Irenaean terms such as *regulam, canon, hypothesis, argumentum*, and others, see Hefner, 296.

[154] See Behr, *Irenaeus*, 78-9, 105-6, and 112-14.

[155] Behr, *Irenaeus*, 113.

Irenaeus and Orthodox Apologetic Methodology

the Law and the Prophets in the covenant delivered at the coming of the Lord."[156] In other words, the canon is the concord and symphony, which is to say the coherent system delivered according to the epistemological principle of revelation and maintained in the Church. There is thus a necessary relationship mutually implicating *hypothesis*, *canon*, and system in each other. This corresponds well to the apologetically oriented position of Clark, who states: "Instead of a series of disconnected propositions, truth will be a rational [read: coherent] system... And each part will derive its significance from the whole."[157] It is precisely because of this that he concludes: "Consequently, if Christianity is to be defended against the objections of other philosophies, the only adequate method will be comprehensive."[158] This well describes Irenaeus' methodology, for in keeping in mind the *hypothesis* and *canon* of the heretics, his treatment of their system is rendered a treatment performed precisely in terms of its comprehensive nature as a system.

Hypothesis, *canon*, and their consequent system being vital to Irenaeus' notion of apologetics, one way of conceiving of this is via the notion of *interconceptuality*, which is to say the notion which takes account of the mutually informing interrelations between concepts. This, in a manner of speaking, is what worldview is, the web of interconceptual relations constituting the subjective act of viewing the world. Moreover, this is also fundamentally what system is, with its implicate

---

[156] Clement, *Strom.* 6.15.125.3, quoted in Behr, *Irenaeus*, 114.
[157] Clark, 24-5.
[158] Clark, 25.

Irenaeus and Orthodox Apologetic Methodology

hypothesis and *canon*. System is thus the web of interrelationships binding concepts which mutually inform each other and, as such, system exists as a totality of concepts (though not in the sense of a numerical sum) and, considered from the point of view of apologetic methodology, must be dealt with in its totality. No concept exists in isolation, and thus interconceptuality is a vital component of apologetic methodology.

Irenaeus time and again demonstrates this principle via his express intention to overthrow the entirety of the false gnostic system, and as shown above it is the lack of access to this interconceptual *hypothesis-canon*-system complex which according to him is the reason for the inability of his predecessors, despite their excellence, to overthrow the gnostic system. It is not a "piecemeal apologetic" which suffices itself to argue a point in atomic isolation, but rather seeks to address the error in its global interconceptuality, to wound and kill the whole beast from all sides by dismantling its genetic code, which is to say its *hypothesis* and *canon*.[159] His critical analysis thus apperceives the whole rather than a string of disparate doctrines. It would actually make no sense for him to speak of its *regulam* if it were otherwise.[160]

---

[159] Bahnsen, *Van Til*, 267.

[160] This also provides a perspective on how Florovsky can say: "As strange as it may appear, one can indeed say: dogmas arise, dogmas are established, but they do not develop. And once established, a dogma is perennial and already an immutable 'rule of faith' [*régula fideï*; 'ο κανών της πίστεως']." See Florovsky, *Creation and Redemption*, (Belmont, MA: Nordland Publishing, 1976), 30. For canon in relation to that which emerges from it is not some development superadded as though a new revelation, but something intrinsic

Irenaeus and Orthodox Apologetic Methodology

Since this is in important ways similar to the guiding and principle focus of Presuppositional Apologetics, which is to say the method of doing apologetics by aiming explicitly at the level of a system's *hypothesis* and *regulam*, its interconceptual presuppositions, it will be worthwhile to consider this aspect of Presuppositional Apologetics in a little more detail so as to shed light on this shared aspect of Irenaeus' methodology. Bahnsen, in analyzing Van Til's views on the matter, states: "a person's theory of knowledge (epistemology) is but part (or an aspect) of a whole network of presuppositions that he maintains, which includes beliefs about the nature of reality (metaphysics) and his norms for living (ethics)."[161] In other words, each informs the other, for each intrinsically depends on the other for their maintenance, and so it is into this interconceptual space that apologetics enters. The failure to do this is to fail to address the actual apologetical problem. Illustrating further Van Til's insight into conceptual interrelatedness, Bahnsen continues:

> Consider someone's commitment to a certain method of knowing (learning, reasoning, proving, etc.). [Not merely *descriptive*]... Rather, the method will be treated as *normative* - as the proper and obligatory way in which to gain and justify knowledge. It carries prescriptive force, then, and becomes a standard for evaluating or judging claims to knowledge. The choice of such an epistemological norm and the choice to

---

to the canon itself. Thus, as dogmas "arise" and are "established," there is simultaneously another sense in which no new dogma is ever in principle possible, for the "entire fullness of truth is already contained in this apophatic vision" (ibid).

[161] Bahnsen, *Van Til*, 263.

> conform in particular cases to it are part of a person's broader lifestyle, reflecting his ultimate authority for conduct and attitudes (ethics). Moreover, a commitment to this particular method of knowing already assumes certain beliefs about the nature of reality (metaphysics).[162]

The import of interconceptuality is clear, for a way of knowing implies a way of knowing *something*, and that something has some sort of metaphysical status, which is to say an idea or intuition about the nature or non-nature of that thing, and these *together* inform ethical norms regarding the how of acting in relation to the (metaphysical) *thing* that is (epistemologically) *known*. The manner in which this relates to Irenaeus' apologetic methodology actually helps to illuminate and clarify the charge of madness he applies to those beset by error. If one's epistemology and metaphysics are intrinsic to one's ethics, then to the degree that one is committed to a false knowing and a false object, to that degree will one's ethics be or become proportionately false, consequently blaspheming God and "resisting and opposing his own salvation" in very principle, as Irenaeus observes to be the two universally common features of all heresy.[163] According to Irenaeus, blasphemy and denial of the principle of salvation, though conceptually distinct, go hand in hand. The consequence of this for apologetic methodology, according to Van Til, as Bahnsen observes and as Irenaeus would seem to agree, is that it "will not be possible, then, to

---

[162] Bahnsen, 263.
[163] *AH*, III.I.2.

resolve disputes of a basic epistemological character between individuals without engaging in argumentation at the level of presupposed worldviews as a whole."[164] In other words, with the consequences thus entailed, because of the necessary interconceptual relationship between a *hypothesis*, *canon*, and system *cum* worldview: "Either one holds the entire system of orthodox Christianity... or one denies the entire system."[165]

To contextualize the above in terms of Scripture, thickening the present discourse with a Scriptural image and moreover showing that Irenaeus is not deviating from but operating according to Scripture by proceeding in the manner he does, it is worth noting that Paul states in his second letter to the Corinthians:

> For the weapons of our warfare are not carnal but mighty in God for pulling down (καθαίρεσις) strongholds (ὀχύρωμα), casting down (καθαιρέω) *arguments* (λογισμός) and every high thing (ὕψωμα) that exalts itself against the knowledge (γνῶσις) of God, bringing every thought (νόημα) into captivity to the obedience of Christ... "Do you look at things according to the outward appearance (πρόσωπον)?[166]

If the foregoing can be taken at the very least as a Scriptural icon or emblem of the Christian approach to apologetics, from it can be evoked certain key elements of a methodology

---

[164] Bahnsen, 263.
[165] Van Til in Bahnsen, 267.
[166] 2 Corinthians 10:4-5, 7.

consistent with that employed by Irenaeus. For instance, one of these elements is found in the repetition of the cognates, καθαίρεσις and καθαιρέω. These carry the sense of demolishing, where in New Testament usage the former is also set in rhetorical contrast to edification,[167] and the latter, connected as it is with λογισμός, indicates that it is in direct relation to defeating argumentation, what *Thayer's Greek Lexicon* describes as "the subtle reasoning of opponents likened to a fortress," and as such is indicating that refutation be aimed at the very structure of their thought, their νόημα, a term which can indicate both thought and the thinking mind itself.[168]

Moreover, to drive the point more firmly towards the notion of a "systems" *canon*, which is to say the interconceptual network of presuppositions, Paul's use of the term πρόσωπον indicates that argumentation is to proceed beyond the surface, what in argumentation could be identified as the secondary levels of claim and counterclaim, and what Van Til was above noted to have described as "piecemeal apologetics."[169] Rather, it is to the stronghold and the bulwark that the argumentation is to advance its attack, with "the weapons of our warfare." The

---

[167] See 2 Corinthians 10:8 and 13:10.

[168] <http://www.blueletterbible.org/lang/lexicon/lexicon.cfm?Strongs=G2507&t=NKJV>, April 25, 2015.

[169] The New Testament usage of *prosopon* does not generally carry the full development of Patristic reflection subsequent to the great Christological and Trinitarian debates of the Fourth Century and beyond. Though not an exhaustive list, for Pauline usage see also 1 Corinthians 13:12, 14:25, 2 Corinthians 3:7, 13, 18, 4:6, 5:12, 11:20, Galatians 1:22, 2:11, Colossians 2:1, 1 Thessalonians 2:17, 3:10. The context of 2 Corinthians 10:7 is clearly an indication of going beyond superficiality.

Pauline symbolism of warfare (στρατεία) applied to argumentation certainly intensifies the sense of strategic battle. And so, extending the analogy, rather than merely attacking the soldiery, it is the stronghold itself that is to be torn down, razed to the ground, for *that* is the object of argumentation. In this sense the soldiery are defeated almost as a mere consequence, their arguments vanishing in smoke as the system which animated them is overthrown. With this in view it seems that Irenaeus is also in concert with and operating according to a Biblical notion of argumentation, and together the authority of this methodology is enhanced.

A NEOPATRISTIC PRESUPPOSITIONAL CRITIQUE OF REFORMED PRESUPPOSITIONALISM

In light of the above, and asserting a distinction from Reformed Presuppositionalism, this section discusses how what might be called Orthodox or Neopatristic Presuppositionalism actually overturns the Reformed version precisely through the intrinsic arbitrariness of Sola Scriptura. The Church's four ontological marks, as per the Creed, are oneness, holiness, catholicity, and apostolicity. Right scriptural hermeneutics require this one, holy, catholic, and apostolic Church as an authoritative interpreter, and in distancing themselves from authoritarian Papism, the Protestants and Reformers through inevitable, rampant, and fractious denominationalism went so far as to unravel the unity of the Church, the Church who as the Body of Christ (Col 1:24) is also the pillar and ground of the truth (1Tit

3:15). By disintegrating the Church, they rendered its rightful interpretive role impossible.

The Reformers manifestly created a strawman by asserting the Bible as supremely authoritative, for the real question was always who has the authority to *interpret* it. Texts require readers, and the Bible as a text requires a human to read and evaluate its contents, an act which always implies tradition or diachronic meaning.[170] The text itself implies the Church as its requisite context, therefore it is hermeneutically absurd to declare that it is purely self-interpreting. One may assert that Scripture is used in order to interpret Scripture, but a person must be involved in the process in order to interpret and compare Scripture with Scripture, and more specifically an orthodox Christian within the orthodox Church. Since individual persons, including Popes and Patriarchs, are fallible, it is the visible Church *as a whole* which declares orthodoxy.[171]

The Scriptures are "what" a Christian trusts, and the Church is "who" a Christian trusts. God did not speak His Word without a voice, and the Church is His voice. If one cannot trust the Church, then they cannot trust the very Body which produced, preserved, and handed down the Scriptures. God must speak authoritatively through both in order to escape solipsism and encounter meaning.

---

[170] For a discussion of the role of tradition in hermeneutic acts, see Joshua Schooping, "John of Damascus and Christian Discourse: The Dialectica Viewed as a Neopatristic Metastructure in Light of Florovsky, Gadamer, and Ricoeur," *International Journal of Orthodox Theology*, 7/3 2016.

[171] "... My Church, and the gates of Hades shall not prevail against it [the Church]" (Mat 16:18).

Irenaeus and Orthodox Apologetic Methodology

To create a hard dualism between the Scriptures and the Church would be a deep misunderstanding about the way in which God works and reveals Himself. The Scriptures are written by the Church; they are *of* the Church, her royal robe and signet, the brightness of her eye. They are the substance, so to speak, of Tradition, where Tradition is understood as the living, diachronic substance of the Church's Scriptural voice. In this sense, the Scriptures are the Church's voice as much as they are God's, her Word as much as His, just as a melody is as much from the instrument as from the musician. It makes little sense to say one trusts the musician and the melody but then not trust his instrument or his use thereof.

The Church, as the Body of Christ, like an instrument, is an ontological extension of His voice. It is the Church's voice that speaks the Word of God, just as it is the Word of God that speaks the Church. Therefore the Church can proclaim with authority, with the voice of Christ that which concerns the weight and meaning of Scripture. One may push the argument into the gray areas of Tradition vs. tradition, creedal faith vs. theologoumena, but to wrest the God-breathed authority from the Church's voice is to dismantle the very reality through which Christ extends Himself into time and space.

This is therefore why one must presuppose the hermeneutic authority of the one, holy, catholic, and apostolic Church, for to do otherwise is to put the very pillar and ground of the truth "in the dock." Since the Scriptures and the Church form a coextensive unity, to question the Church is to question God's Word, to separate that which God made one. The Church is the world, the horizon, in which the Scriptures have their existence, and Tradition the breath of her Scriptural mouth.

No amount of argumentation on behalf of the authority of Scripture will escape the present argument, for the present argument presupposes the authority of Scripture. Church and Scripture are two necessary truths, for just as Scripture presupposes the Church as her instrumental author and authoritative interpreter, likewise the Church presupposes Scripture as the Word of her Lord, spoken to her and through her. Thus breaking the solipsistic hermeneutic circle, the Church is the hermeneutic key unlocking the treasures of Scripture. Christ, working through the synodality of the Orthodox Church, guards and guides her to authentic transpersonal meaning and preserves her binding authority.

Not an individual, nor an invisible Church,[172] every time a person stands over and above the Church's interpretation in order to interpret Scripture with Scripture alone, they place themselves as judges of the Church's witness, which is to say they stand outside the Church. In their view, there is finally no interpreter who is more authoritative than the individual, whether they intend this as a consequence or not. The only other option is to interpret within the Church. Yet, as a consequence of the Reformed trivialization of the Church's authority, those who stand outside the Church in order to interpret Scripture are likewise outside of Christ, and thereby forfeit all hermeneutic authority. In pointing to Scripture alone one ends up pointing on the basis of one's personal exegetical

---

[172] Invisible churches cannot affirm or declare anything, and merely stand as a rhetorical place-holders.

prowess to oneself alone as the arbiter of truth. The question is therefore not whether the Scriptures are supremely authoritative, but who has the authority to rightly divide the word of truth (2Tim 2:15) contained therein.

The Scriptures are sufficiently complex that the possibility of error is always present, and it is historically incontestable that heresies very often cite Scripture. The question is: Who has the authority to interpret Scripture and thus resolve the inevitable differences of interpretation that arise? Clearly the authority is not a Christian in isolation, nor a Church hierarch per se, but always the Church as such considered as a whole. As mentioned above, the Church's ontological marks are oneness, holiness, catholicity, and (diachronic) apostolicity, and in this light all interpretive acts must bear the signature of these if they are to carry any authority. If they lack these marks, then whatever is left, however true, is not properly of the Church, which is to say of Christ. In this sense, one can hold to many Christian truths, and yet still remain outside of the ark of the Church.

To reduce historic Christianity and, in essence, all other Christians into mere influences in one's Scriptural exegesis, one has demeaned the Church and made a caricature of orthodoxy, fashioning it in the image of one's own best reading. No one is left to be an authority but oneself. Yet, truth is not something to be held merely individually and in the abstract, but in living communion with the Body of Christ. Since anyone can in principle take several Scriptural verses which have some commonality and on their basis form a novel doctrine, some process more than reading Scripture alone must be present, for what mechanism is left in order to arbitrate competing interpretations if not the Church? Clearly someone is persuading and being persuaded, yet something more than persuasiveness must present itself; there must be an authority lest doctrinal agnosticism prevail. If the one, holy, catholic, and apostolic Church does not have the authority to arbitrate in these matters, then all that is left is an individualistic or sectarian hermeneutic vacuum. This is the inextricable problem of all Protestant, Evangelical, and Reformed ecclesiologies: they cannot become one;[173] they cannot become catholic;[174] they cannot become apostolic.[175]

It can also be noted, contra Papism, that the Bishop, including the Patriarch, has the highest teaching and administrative authority in the Church, but this does not mean the Bishop is himself equivalent to the Church considered as a whole, or infallible over it. The bishops, each occupying the "chair" of Peter, are the chief servants. It is the Church, however, essentially synodal, which is the total authority, and which receives the sacred promises. For example, it is the notion of ecumenicality in the ecumenical councils which guarantees their authority, not the fact that one or another bishop was

---

[173] This is clear from the endless variation that is denominationalism, often resulting in vastly different confessions, each, of course, derived *Sola Scriptura*.

[174] This becomes impossible, at the very least, as a result of the first. They can become pluralistic, which is evidenced by the modern ecumenical movement, but this is not the same as oneness or universality.

[175] Only in the most tortured sense can Protestant, Evangelical, and Reformed "traditions" claim apostolicity, for it must be completely dehistoricized and reduced to apostolic doctrine - derived in principle independently of tradition - rather than an actual, unbroken, and historic chain of transmission from one living Christian to another.

present. It is the Church which speaks as a whole, a voice which cannot be programmatically reduced to a single voice. This is how Neopatristic Presuppositionalism also distinguishes itself from Papism, for Papism distorts authority by reducing it to an individual. By reducing or narrowing authority from the Church to an individual who stands supreme over the Church, synodality is lost. This situation distorts the proper balance of ecclesiology, for no matter how pious or righteous any Pope or Patriarch may be, no matter how consistent or correct his decisions, no matter how venerable his wisdom, it changes the basic vision of the Church to centralize authority, or decentralize authority, via a single individual. The Church is fundamentally, ontologically synodal.

    Returning to the hermeneutic problem of *sola scriptura*, it ends in a sort of hermeneutic solipsism, for there is no possibility of appealing to anyone. Thus, whether Luther had it right, or Calvin, or Zwingli, no one can even in principle know because the only thing with which to confirm or disconfirm their views is some individual reader of Scripture. Everything other than the exact phraseology of a Scriptural book is opinion; all interpretation is opinion. *Sola scriptura* ultimately makes Scripture impossible to interpret, and so the fact that Scripture is interpreted all the time by them demonstrates that they are constantly contradicting themselves. Since some of the most important Christian doctrines are implicit in Scripture rather than explicit, the unpacking of them is the product of fallible human reading, irresolvable communally for the community carries no real hermeneutic authority. It would be impossible therefore to have confidence in the belief that Jesus is God, or that God is Triune, for each of these doctrines are the result of individual hermeneutic acts and not merely straight readings from Scripture. Each individual reader would in principle have to recreate the entire theological tradition, for why one would believe, say, a Nicene position rather than an Arian one is constantly open to debate, for the Church as Church is unable to settle the matter conclusively.

Rather than developing a piecemeal argument against *sola scriptura*, the current study's focus on Presuppositional Apologetics seeks naturally to understand the basic presuppositions inherent in their position. Keith Mathison, a Protestant defender of *sola scriptura*, states: "Roman Catholic and Orthodox apologists have been effective in their criticisms in large part because of the fact that most Protestants have adopted a subjective and individualistic version of sola scriptura that bears little resemblance to the doctrine of the Reformers."[176] One presupposition here is that "the doctrine of the Reformers" is able to carry *any* type of authority, for he is clearly stating that something ought to resemble their doctrine, that they represent some type of group who maintained the proper conclusion. Why else refer to it? Without the Reformers

---

[176] Keith Mathison, *The Shape of Sola Scriptura*, (Moscow, ID: Canon Press, 2001), 14. Of course, this is the exact predicted consequence of *sola scriptura*, and the irony of the appeal to *traditional* Reformed doctrine is apparently lost. His immediate recourse is to *tradition*, the very thing he states carries no weight. Yet, the fact that this is perhaps a natural reaction to and consequence of Papism must also be acknowledged. When a centrist, as opposed to a synodal, ecclesiology overclaims power, *sola scriptura* perhaps seems a viable path of escape.

as a type of standard, all that is left is his *personal* exegetical and rhetorical prowess. Clearly, Mathison is appealing to *tradition*.

Doctrine is intrinsically interpretive in nature, and in this way the very notion of doctrine itself presupposes tradition, and in his case Reformed tradition, for tradition is the only thing that can sustain doctrine. Without tradition there is no mechanism for maintaining the "implicit" doctrines of Scripture. The complaint that *sola scriptura* unjustly collapses into some type of *solo scriptura* is therefore a complaint that the Reformed position, i.e. tradition, equally open to debate, is failing to be maintained properly. He thus will seek to go back to history and Scripture in order to persuade his readers that the *traditional* Reformed doctrine is the right reading of Scripture. If he states that the Church is authoritative, that historic orthodoxy is binding, then he is clearly suffering from an attempt at trying to both have his cake and eat it, too, to both secure all the benefits of tradition while at the same time denying both the authority of tradition and the one, holy, catholic, and apostolic Church's ability to make authoritative and binding statements of faith. Even the doctrine of *sola scriptura* is itself a tradition, along with the other four "*solas*."

A supremely authoritative object requires a supremely authoritative view. Neopatristic presuppositionalism therefore exposes the inadequacy of, and provides the needed correction to, Reformed presuppositionalism. It asserts both the supreme authority of the Scriptures while at the same time holding forth the Church's supreme interpretive authority of these Scriptures. It also provides ground for faith in the Church's doctrine, and a context in which the Scriptures can be interpreted in consistently faithful, rather than ceaselessly fractioning, ways. Orthodox Presuppositionalism answers the question: By what authority is an *interpretation* of Scripture maintained?

PROSPECTUS AND CONCLUSION

Though much, much more could be said about Irenaeus' apologetic methodology, a key first step has been made to identify certain key foundational features. It is defensive, demonstrative, and offensive; it is presuppositional and systematic, which is to say, it identifies worldviews and addresses a system's *hypothesis* and *canon* as an interconceptual whole. It treats extensively with the opposing sides' positions, seeking to expose that which remains concealed behind a veil of plausible words, which is to say it employs a type of hermeneutic of suspicion and critical analysis regarding that which operates according to a false *canon*. It identifies (the) two universal features implicit in heresy: blasphemy and denial of salvation. Moreover, it considers issues of persuasion as secondary to destruction of the false system, and as such is largely intra-ecclesial, an observation which illustrates the protective and strengthening motives inherent in Irenaeus' methodology. It has also been observed that Irenaeus' apologetic methodology operates according to its own *hypothesis* and *canon*, and it uses this to both recognize and evaluate the falseness of the opposing system together with its *hypothesis* and *canon*, and moreover to establish the truth of the orthodox *canon* of truth. It also appears to mandate the doing of apologetics, an activity which it sees as appropriate for any who would diligently and faithfully read Irenaeus' text, a text which he intends to be studied carefully for the increased development of apologetics. It is also rational and intends to be rationally coherent and philosophically intelligible.

Moreover, Irenaeus sees apologetics as protecting against the corruption of the faith and the captivity of the faithful to deception by exposing error, refuting error, and defending truth. It strengthens the faithful as a pedagogical consideration by furnishing its readers the means by which they too can learn to oppose error and defend truth, establishing, moreover, rational grounds on which to stabilize those who are neophytes in the faith - intentionally constituting a textbook for these purposes. It also hopes and prays for, following upon the complete destruction of the false system, the conversion and salvation of those caught in the scheme of the Enemy, indicating an ethical imperative and deep spiritual dimension to apologetics that transcends "merely academic" concerns.

Though, as was said above, only a beginning has been made, albeit hopefully substantial and warranting continued development, further areas of study include, in addition to a deeper study of Irenaeus from a continued apologetics perspective, appraisals of the methodologies of other key Church Fathers, as well as the work of contemporary apologists in terms relevant to the present field.[177] Furthermore, the role of Scripture specifically as a tool of apologetics needs to be further

---

[177] See Appendix 1 for a brief, indicative study of how Athanasius and Gregory of Nyssa may be brought to bear on the present study of Irenaeus' apologetic methodology.

explored. Also, only introduced above, a fuller elaboration of the manner in which philosophical considerations inform Christian apologetics, such as those emerging from the Christian (which is to say Christological) worldview, (theistic and Trinitarian) metaphysics, (revelational and Christological) epistemology, ethics, hermeneutics, etc., in order to answer, together with Scripture and Tradition (including such things as the Ecumenical Councils), questions such as what, say, metaphysical and epistemological commitments are entailed if not necessitated by revelation and catholic, Apostolic, and Ecumenical Tradition. These are key for assessing, addressing, and perhaps exposing and overthrowing the *hypothesis*, *canon*, and system of the various philosophical systems and worldviews being elaborated today.

Though the present study did not seek an extensive evaluation of the other primary methods of contemporary disciplines of apologetics, there seems to be a certain affinity with elements of the presuppositional approach as well as with the Classical (with its resemblance to the Catholic) approach, and as Irenaeus is observed to make arguments from history it would also seem that Evidentialism has some place at the Irenaean table. Given that Irenaeus is such a foundational Father of the Church, it moreover seems that his attitude towards apologetics extends beyond him, entering at least potentially into the theological continuum that is Orthodoxy. With many points of contact with the other methods, the Irenaean *cum* Orthodox method of apologetics will also find that it differs from them as well, an issue which also deserves further treatment.

Irenaeus and Orthodox Apologetic Methodology

Finally, Irenaeus the apologist has been shown to offer meaningful guidance concerning apologetic methodology. Despite what further work needs to be accomplished, the present field of apologetics can be treated as open to Orthodox Christians such that they can more fully enter into apologetic activity in a self-consistently Orthodox manner, for at no time is the defense of the canon of truth unnecessary. Irenaeus lived in a pluralistic culture, and as such his vigorous and extensive method of apologetics serves even more appropriately as a potential model for the Church as it wades through the intellectual waters of the contemporary world. According to Irenaeus, the Church needs apologetics for itself, for its faithful, and with Irenaeus' robust method of apologetics the Church can critically engage with those who seek to persuade with plausible words according to a false canon, exposing their error and overthrowing it in hopes that the Church be strengthened and those chastened by exposure and defeat might "stand away from the void, and relinquish the shadow," cease from blasphemy and self-destruction, and thereby repent and be converted to the Gospel, the truth.

APPENDIX 1
A BRIEF EXCURSUS INDICATING ATHANASIUS AND GREGORY OF NYSSA'S CONTINUITY WITH IRENAEUS' APOLOGETIC METHODOLOGY

Though there is not space to thoroughly mine subsequent Church Fathers, a very brief excursus treating of Athanasius' and Gregory of Nyssa's apologetic efforts will go some way towards indicating whether or not Irenaeus' apologetic methodology coheres with other foundational Church Fathers, at the very least with the intention of indicating a promising direction for further research into the matter. Another reason for looking at these two in particular is due to their relationship with key moments of the Church's historical development. Succinctly, Irenaeus is Ante-Nicene, Athanasius is Nicene, and Gregory is Post-Nicene. In other words, their position relative to the Council of Nicaea provides a useful framework for identifying any potential continuity of motives and methodology. Therefore, if there is an apologetic methodology which emerges prior to Nicaea, continues during Nicaea, and persists beyond Nicaea, and, moreover, in key Church Fathers, then the claim that there is such a thing as an *Orthodox* apologetic methodology becomes that much more tenable.

Briefly, it is observed that Athanasius' *Against the Heathen* is suffused with ample and explicit reference to argumentation, proof, demonstration, refutation, etc., as well as to the necessity of these.[178] These are often undertaken in

---

[178] Cf. Athanasius, *Against the Heathen*, tr. Archibald Robertson, Nicene and Post-Nicene Fathers, Second Series, vol. 4. ed. Philip Schaff and Henry Wace,

Irenaeus and Orthodox Apologetic Methodology

reference to proving God's oneness as well as the existence of the soul, but also to seeks out to disprove idolatry and false concepts of Deity, at times using their own ideas as refutations against them, and also charging them with impiety (linked with madness).[179] In short, this work of Athanasius' demonstrates that his apologetic methodology is consistent in important respects to that of Irenaeus, though it is certainly nowhere near as thorough. Relying often on Scripture, he identifies, examines, and seeks to refute the false Arian system as a whole, and demonstrates the reasonableness of the fundamentals of the Christian system. He does much the same thing in his *Discourses against the Arians*, addressing moreover the notion of falsehood's deceptive nature along with the need to expose it, casting proof at them from all sides, and overcoming them with argumentation.[180] He also refutes with a hope to elicit their repentance.[181] He expresses especial concern to secure the faithful.[182] He also proceeds in a similar fashion in his *Letters to Serapion*.[183] In short, though at the moment only the barest

---

(Buffalo, NY: Christian Literature Publishing Co., 1892), 1.7; 6.3; 7.3; 11.2; 16.1, 6; 18.1; 19.4, 24.1; 27.3, 5; 28.2, 3; 29.2; 30.1, 4; 32.1, 3; 38.2, 4; 40.1, 6; 45.3; 46.2.

[179] Ibid. 11.2; 25.2,4; 28-9; 32.3; 33.1, 36:1, 3; 40.1.

[180] Athanasius, *Discourses Against the Arians*, tr. John Henry Newman and Archibald Robertson, Nicene and Post-Nicene Fathers, Second Series, vol. 4. ed. Philip Schaff and Henry Wace, (Buffalo, NY: Christian Literature Publishing Co., 1892), 1.1, 8, and 10.

[181] Ibid. 2.1.

[182] Ibid. 3.1.

[183] Though the following list does not exhaust all that Athanasius has to say reflecting on his notion of apologetic methodology, but if perused carefully its contents will furnish ample evidence for a shared set of concerns with Irenaeus. See *Letters to Serapion on the Holy Spirit*, tr. Mark DelCogliano, Andrew Radde-Gallwitz, and Lewis Ayres, in *Works on the Spirit: Athanasius the*

Irenaeus and Orthodox Apologetic Methodology

surface can be scratched concerning Athanasius' methodology, he confirms and by no means contradicts a continuity of apologetic methodology.

Concerning Gregory of Nyssa, much the same is the case. The books against Eunomius are a great example of a thorough engagement with the ideas held by the opposing party together with a philosophically coherent refutation. After defending against the slanderous charges made by Eunomius, distinguishing them from blasphemy and asserting a methodology of proof,[184] he also sees a hierarchy of Eunomius' views such that to deal with the weightier is to automatically deal with the less weighty.[185] Gregory demonstrates awareness of Eunomius' views as a system of beliefs, one which in order to defeat he will meticulously go through his words, scrutinize them, and "repeat his statements one by one" so as to answer to all the charges.[186] He moreover charges Eunomius with inventing new words, departing from tradition, "abandoning the inspired terms," and inventing a system of grammatical trivialities.[187] Gregory also shows awareness of the notion of a starting-point for argumentation, a conception of methodology for proof, as well as the relatively normative use of logic in establishing one's

---

Great and Didymus the Blind, (Yonkers, NY: St Vladimir's Press, 2011), 1.1.4, 1.2.2, 1.2.5, 1.2.6, 1.3.2, 1.10.4, 1.10.5, 1.15.1, 1.16.1, 1.18.4, 1.19.1, 1.20.4, 1.21.4, 1.24.5, 1.27.4, 1.28.1, 1.28.2, 1.32.1, 1.33.2, 1.33.6, 2.1.1, 2.7.1, 2.7.2, 2.11.1, 2.13.1, 2.16.4, 3.1.1, 3.1.2, 3.7.1.

[184] Gregory of Nyssa, *Contra Eunomius*, tr. W. Moore, H.A. Wilson, and H.C. Ogle, Nicene and Post-Nicene Fathers, Second Series, Vol. 5. ed. Philip Schaff and Henry Wace, (Buffalo, NY: Christian Literature Publishing Co., 1893), I.13.

[185] Ibid, I.13; VIII.1.

[186] Ibid, I.13, I.18, I.19; VI. 1.

[187] Ibid, I.14; III.1.

Irenaeus and Orthodox Apologetic Methodology

views.[188] Gregory also affirms that it is normative for argumentation to proceed from the more basic premise, truth, or axiom, and advance to the more doubtful so that it can be "legitimately deduced."[189] Failure to do this, as he charges of Eunomius, is merely "proving the obscure by the obscure."[190] His defeat of Eunomius' arguments he characterizes by declaring that "his view is unfounded, and lacks a principle: it starts from data that are not granted, and then it constructs by mere logic a blasphemy upon them."[191] In this sense he also attacks the sophistic use of logic and reason.

Gregory also distances his argument from rhetoric, as well as from fanciness of dialectic, and asserts that the strength of his reasoning flows from its first principle, "the very Word Himself."[192] Moreover, the inconsistency of Eunomius' argument, considering "his statement in light of his own words," ends in his own self-refutation and the defeat of his "phantom doctrine," where logical consistency is the litmus test of truth claims.[193] Gregory moreover uses Eunomius' words to support his own arguments, appealing simultaneously to piety and reason.[194] Examples of this sort could be multiplied almost at will, and as such, even only looking as far as Gregory's *Contra Eunomius*, it is clear that there are deep affinities with Irenaeus,

---

[188] Ibid, I.18.
[189] Ibid, I.18.
[190] Ibid, I.18.
[191] Ibid, I.19.
[192] Ibid, III.1.
[193] Ibid, III.1.
[194] Ibid, VI.4.

from identifying his opponent, to working carefully and methodologically through the opponent's system, identifying the system of truth, overthrowing error from within, proceeding via rational demonstration and proof, etc. As such it would be superfluous to go through more of his texts, though it is worth mentioning that *On the Holy Spirit: Against the Followers of Macedonius, On the Holy Trinity, and of the Godhead of the Holy Spirit, On 'Not Three Gods,' On the Making of Man, On the Soul and the Resurrection*, and especially the *Great Catechism*, will all more than amply reward a further study of Orthodox apologetic methodology, and moreover show a continuity with that which has been shown in Irenaeus' works.[195]

---

[195] These texts can all be found in the same volume with *Contra Eunomius*.

APPENDIX 2
CONTRA LESSING: A CRITICAL EXAMINATION OF LESSING'S DITCH

"Lessing's ditch" is named after a phrase penned by Gotthold Lessing, an 18th Century German dramaturgist, philosopher, and freemason.[196] Emerging within the period of the German Enlightenment and German Idealism, Lessing's ditch has in a manner of speaking reflected the spirit of his age.[197] As a "problem" it has travelled widely and fascinated many, from Coleridge to Kierkegaard.[198] One recent author has said that today "Lessing's ditch is as deep as it ever was."[199] It has also perhaps been a reef involved in the shipwreck of many people's faith in traditional teachings concerning the Christ of history and of faith. The issue of the disjointed relationship between history and theology is still active today, and Lessing's ditch, as a conceptual image and a philosophical argument expressing this disjointedness, is an important touchstone for approaching the contemporary question of how to understand and address this relationship.[200]

---

[196] Henry Chadwick, *Lessing's Theological Writings*, (Stanford: Stanford University Press: 1967), 9, 28.

[197] Toshimasa Yasukata, *Lessing's Philosophy of Religion and the German Enlightenment*, (Oxford, 2002), 3.

[198] Gordon Michaelson, Jr., *Lessing's "Ugly Ditch": A Study of Theology and History*, (University Park: Pennsylvania State University Press, 1985), 2-3.

[199] Michael Kruger, *Canon Revisited: Establishing the Origins and Authority of the New Testament Books*, (Wheaton: Crossway: 2012), 22.

[200] Though not repeatable here, much work has been done on Lessing's relationship to the Enlightenment, to Idealism, and to thinkers such as Spinoza, Leibniz, and others. For Lessing in historical context see Henry Allison, *Lessing and the Enlightenment: His Philosophy of Religion and its Relation to Eighteenth-Century Thought*, (Ann Arbor: University of Michigan Press.

Irenaeus and Orthodox Apologetic Methodology

The present essay will examine Lessing's ditch especially through the lens of his use of a quote from Origen's *Contra Celsum*, a quote which appears at the opening of Lessing's pamphlet and is mentioned in three subsequent paragraphs. This quote serves as a recurring 'proof text' for Lessing's argument inasmuch as it concerns the role of the presence or absence of the supernatural as evidence for or against the truth claims of Christian theology inasmuch as they are rooted in history. A major question to be addressed is whether or not Lessing adequately reflects this thought of Origen, and in what way this impacts Lessing's overall argument.[201] Following this, a critical examination of some of the major themes which emerged in the first part will be examined more closely to see whether or not Lessing's ditch is or is not an actual "problem."

What is Lessing's basic argument?

Lessing's basic argument, his "ditch," is a perceived impasse between facts of history and truths of reason.[202] Lessing,

---

1966). See also: *The Cambridge Companion to German Idealism*; ed. Ameriks, Karl; (Cambridge: Cambridge University Press, 2000).

[201] Outside the scope of this study, it is yet significant that Lessing is known to have been antagonistic to Christian orthodoxy, anonymously published the "Reimarus Fragments" to this effect, and was even expressly interested in its division and demise. See Chadwick's Introduction, esp. 13-14. Also, on behalf of Freemasonry, in *Ernst and Falk* Lessing further wrote on behalf of dividing peoples and groups as a matter of principle. See *Lessing: Philosophical and Theological Writings*, 195. All of this is to say that it is manifestly possible that Lessing was in some sense deliberately engineering his ditch.

[202] Though there is not space here to explore and adopt them, Michalson actually identifies three distinct ditches: a *temporal* ditch between the present and the past, a *metaphysical* ditch between truths of history and truths of theology, and an *existential* ditch between believer and belief. Michalson may be making too much of these divisions, which could introduce problems of

though accepting the historical elements of Christian religious history, asserts that it is categorically unjustified "to make the leap from this historical truth into a quite different class of truths."[203] There is an incommensurable distance between historical truth and the claims of theology. In fact, "however undisputed and indisputable these [historical] reports may be, I do deny that they can and should bind me to the least faith in the other teachings of Christ."[204] Thus, through a mitigation of the persuasive force of history to warrant theology, Lessing yet seeks to accept some of Christ's "other teachings" on "nothing but these teachings themselves,"[205] teachings which he accepts as being compatible with the "necessary truths of reason."[206] The teachings Lessing does not see himself as bound to are those which are concerned with whether or not it is true that "God has a Son who is of the same essence as himself."[207] These, according to Lessing's essay, are due to the combination of history's inability to generate binding truth claims, "since they are merely reports of miracles,"[208] together with an absence of a personal experience of miracle. Since "reports of miracles are

---

their own, for Lessing's ditch functions as a unity, but they are helpful in articulating important facets of what otherwise could appear to be a 'simple' problem. See Michalson, 8-20.

[203] Lessing, 87. Please note that all quotes of Lessing are taken from Gotthold Lessing, *Philosophical and Theological Writings*, ed. Nisbet, H.B., (Cambridge: Cambridge University Press, 2005).

[204] Lessing, 87.

[205] Ibid.

[206] Ibid, 85.

[207] Ibid, 86.

[208] Ibid.

not miracles,"[209] these reports therefore "do not bind [him] to the least faith."[210]

Two types, there are some "other teachings of Christ" which Lessing accepts, and some "other teachings of Christ" which he does not accept.[211] The principle underlying this distinction is that since Christ's claim that He is the Son of God, insofar as it is a mere claim, is only true *as a matter of history concerning claims*, and since the purport of His claim is not a *necessary truth of reason*, Lessing declares it is therefore not binding upon him to believe what his "reason refuses to accept" (Lessing 86), what he calls earlier "incomprehensible truths."[212] In other words, he believes, as a matter of accurate and factual historical record, that Christ *said* He is the Son of God, but the fact that He said this does not and categorically cannot in any sense prove that it is true in substance. Moreover, since it is without a present and empirically verifiable miracle, being that it is otherwise "incomprehensible" to him, it is therefore not necessary for him to affirm anything more than that it is merely a historical utterance - despite the fact that the claim of divinity was itself accepted by Lessing as having been accompanied by authentic miracles and fulfilled prophecies. Moreover, since on this basis these historical truths are not binding, they therefore do not "require" him to "revise" or "change" his "metaphysical and moral concepts," nor his "basic ideas on the nature of the deity."[213] Thus Lessing artfully dispenses with any need or motive to believe Christian theological claims.

---

[209] Ibid, 84.

[210] Ibid, 86. Likewise with prophecy: "Reports of fulfilled prophecies are not fulfilled prophecies" (Lessing 84).

[211] See Lessing 86, 87.

[212] Ibid, 85.

[213] Ibid, 87.

To attempt to put his argument in compact form: 1) The history of the gospels is uncontested; 2) Historical facticity does not necessitate theological consequences; 3) The verification of supernatural evidences requires personal, empirical attestation, which in Lessing's case are absent; *therefore* 4) Lessing sees no need or motive to believe in a theology centered on Christ.

The "ditch," then, is simply an illustration of this basic argument, and according to Lessing it is unleapable because there is a category error: "That is, contingent truths of history can never become the proof of necessary truths of reason."[214] Why? Because the contingent truths of history cannot be rationally demonstrated, merely asserted or reported, and the result is that "if no historical truth can be demonstrated, then nothing can be demonstrated by means of historical truths."[215] Being insufficient for proof, then, history cannot make any conclusive claims about the divine nature of Christ. Therefore, the only thing in this context which is admissible from gospel history are certain of Christ's teachings, "these teachings themselves,"[216] but only insofar as they can be self-attestingly accepted on their own ground as necessary truths of reason.[217]

The Origen of Lessing's Ditch

Dated 1777, just four years prior to his death and when we was more directly involved in disseminating literature against Christianity, Lessing's famous essay, "On the Proof of

---

[214] Ibid, 85. Though he has "earnestly" tried. See Lessing, 87.
[215] Ibid.
[216] Ibid, 87.
[217] As opposed to being accepted on the basis of Christ's personal authority as the Son of God.

the Spirit and of Power," begins with a quotation from Origen's *Contra Celsum*.[218] Since the issue seemingly raised by the quote will recur in Lessing's essay as a pivot around which he establishes his thesis, it will be instructive to look at the quote in question. Taken from *Contra Celsum* I.2, Lessing gives it: "…because of the prodigious miracles which may be proved by this argument among many others, that traces of them still remain among those who live according to the will of the Word."[219] The meaning that Lessing gives the quote is quite clear: "Origen was still in that position [of observing miracles], and he was quite correct in saying that, in this proof of the spirit and of power, the Christian religion had a proof… he had necessarily to acknowledge that proof of the spirit and of power if he did not wish to deny his own senses."[220] In other words, Lessing sees in Origen's statement a reference to "proof" of the "Christian religion" derived from miracle and confirmed by "his own senses."

How else does Lessing utilize Origen in this essay? He says he is no longer in Origen's "position," which is to say he is no longer in a position of observing miracles with his own eyes.[221] In distinguishing himself from Origen, Lessing even says of himself: "I… live in the eighteenth century in which miracles no longer happen." In other words, Origen lived when miracles happened, whereas he, Lessing, does not. Moreover, in that quote it can be noted that Lessing has claimed baldly that miracles simply do not happen in the eighteenth century, a subject which will be discussed more thoroughly below. Later on he speaks of Origen again, saying Origen's "proof," his "argument" for the Christian faith, is "primarily and specifically

---

[218] Lessing, 83.
[219] Ibid, 84.
[220] Ibid.
[221] Ibid.

through the miracles which were still happening then."[222] In other words, Lessing is using Origen to great effect to show that without miracle and, what is more, with an absence of the "proof of the proof," he can legitimately ask, "how can I be expected to believe equally strongly, and with infinitely less cause, those incomprehensible truths which people believed for the strongest *reasons* sixteen to eighteen centuries ago?"[223] It is precisely by denying any contemporary occurrence of miracles, in not seeing them with his own eyes, that he simultaneously denies the ground for believing on the basis of undemonstrable historical truths.[224]

What, however, is Origen himself saying in that quote? What is its context? What is Origen calling a miracle? Is Origen's idea being expressed by Lessing, or is Lessing perhaps misleadingly proof-texting Origen in an act of eisegesis?[225] After looking at the quote in its native context, one will then be in a better position to determine whether Lessing's use of Origen has actual reference to Origen's idea, or whether it is a problematic misuse of the text.

Within the same paragraph of *Contra Celsum*, prior to the phrase quoted by Lessing, Origen contextualizes the statement in question this way: "A man coming to the gospel from Greek conceptions and training would not only judge that it [the fundamental truth of Christianity] was true, but would also put it into practice and so prove it to be correct; and he would complete what seemed to be lacking judged by the criterion of a Greek proof, thus establishing the truth of Christianity." One noteworthy element from Origen's sentence

---

[222] Ibid, 85.

[223] Ibid. Emphasis in this quote, as well as in any subsequent quotes, are mine.

[224] Ibid.

[225] At least one author has noted that Lessing is perhaps being "deceptive" in his arranging of his argument. See Yasukata, 60.

Irenaeus and Orthodox Apologetic Methodology

here is that his notion of proof is intrinsically linked to *practice*. According to Origen, not only would it be judged true if one is coming to the gospel from Greek modes of reasoning, but more so would *prove* it to be true by putting the fundamental truths of Christianity into practice. In fact, in Origen's view there is arguably something incomplete or "lacking" in the knowledge of the truth of Christianity unless it is established in the exercise of these teachings in the context of one's own life.

Origen continues, saying that "the gospel has a proof which is peculiar to itself, and which is more divine than a Greek proof based on dialectical argument." In other words, when Lessing makes reference to the "necessary truths of reason,"[226] and what is more puts this in opposition to the "contingent truths of history," he has just argued to the effect that it is the necessary truths of reason which ought to have the most persuasive power, but as the statement above shows, Origen disagrees and instead argues that there is something "more divine than a proof based on dialectical argument."[227] Thus it is shown that in some sense Lessing, by avoiding the notion of practice, is distancing himself from a proper reading of Origen, implicating Origen's thought in Lessing's own tension, one between history and reason, a tension which is not natural to or consistent with Origen's own thought.

The very next sentence in Origen's *Contra Celsum* is where Lessing derives his quote. Lessing, it should be noted, does not put the full quote. The full quote states: "This more divine demonstration the apostle calls a 'demonstration of the Spirit and of power' [1 Corinthians 2:4]-of spirit because of the prophecies and especially those which refer to Christ, which are capable of convincing anyone who reads them; of power because

---

[226] Lessing, 85.
[227] CC I.2.

of the prodigious miracles which may be proved to have happened by this argument among many others, that traces of them still remain among those who live according to the will of the Logos."[228] Notice that the reference to prophecies is precisely that an argument *from history* is convincing! Origen is saying that in and of themselves, knowledge of the fulfillment of historic prophecies "*are* capable of convincing anyone who reads them." In other words, contrary to Lessing's position, prophetic fulfillment in history is not an obstacle to belief in the supernatural dimension of who Christ is, but is involved instead in a "more divine demonstration"; there is no tension here between the contingent truths of history and the necessary truths of reason. In a sense, the historic prophetic fulfillment is superior to the "necessary truths of reason," that is, if by these is meant something analogous to Origen's notion of "proof based on dialectical argument." It could even be the case that, concerning prophecy at least, there is no place in Origen for Lessing's idea of contingent *prophetic* truths of history.

Moving forward, it is the next part of Origen's statement which Lessing seems to take the most interest in, that part which is concerned with the "power," which is to say the "prodigious miracles."[229] Lessing is motivated to show that since these are not known by him in his own day, then he is therefore justified in not accepting the others as binding. This could seem to be what Origen's own argument indicates, that the truth of Christianity "may be proved to have happened by *this* argument

---

[228] Cf. Romans 1:16: "For I am not ashamed of the gospel, for it is the *power* of God for salvation to everyone who believes." Though there is not space here to enter into a Scriptural exegesis of Paul's notion of divine "power," it ought to at least be noted that it is the gospel, the message itself, which can be understood as identical to the "power" of God. This relates to Origen's emphasis on conversion as proof of Christ.

[229] See above footnote.

Irenaeus and Orthodox Apologetic Methodology

among many others, that traces of them[miracles] still remain among those who live according to the will of the Logos." Thus Lessing, by purporting to show that *this* argument is not verified in the present day by the presence of "prodigious miracles," seems to imply that he can thereby safely dispense with the "many other" arguments concerned with believing in "the other teachings of Christ."[230] The question to be answered here, however, is concerned with discerning more accurately what is meant by Origen here when he speaks of miracles.

Before looking at Origen's understanding of miracle, it ought not go without noticing that Origen says, and Lessing quotes, that miracle is only one argument "among many others." Lessing thus seems to overlook the "contingent" dimension to Origen's argument based on miracle. Lessing also does not take up to discuss the other portion of Origen's quote, which is that these miracles occur in those who "live according to the will of the Logos." There is a direct correspondence, as will be shown below, between miracle and what might be called "holy living." This notion of holy living will actually play an important role in Origen's understanding of miracle, and it is to this that the present paper now turns.

When one begins to dig into Origen's notion of miracle, it does not generally seem that he has in mind exactly what Lessing seems to take from it. For example, though Lessing never clearly defines what he means by miracle, one type of miracle that he seems to have in mind is resurrection, either Christ raising someone from the dead, or Christ's own resurrection.[231] Origen, at least in *Contra Celsum*, though it is doubtworthy he would deny it, does not generally speak of Christ's resurrection as a miracle. He does, however, refer to it

---

[230] Lessing, 86.
[231] Ibid.

as a *doctrine*. In fact, Origen says "the doctrine of the resurrection… is deep and hard to explain, and needs a wise man of advanced skill more than any other doctrine."[232] Origen elsewhere says a similar thing of the resurrection, that it is a doctrine, calling it "our doctrine of the resurrection."[233] Thus it seems that Origen does not find the doctrine of the resurrection to be a self-evident, obvious miracle, but something preeminently difficult and profound, requiring extremely skillful and wise explanation.

At least one time Origen discusses Christ's resurrection as παραδοξότερος,[234] from παράδοξος, which relates to the English word paradox, and so it is not quite the same as the Greek terms which are generally rendered as "miracle," such as σημεῖον, which can also be translated as "sign," and δύναμις, which can also be translated as "power."[235] What this indicates is that the primary "miracle" of Christ mentioned by Lessing, that of His resurrection, is not so much a miracle for Origen, but a difficult and lofty doctrine. This is not to deny the use of the word miracle to Lessing, or to Origen, but to show that there is a certain fuzziness and artful ambiguity in Lessing's argument. He neither defines nor offers a clear scope to miracle, making only mention of resurrection, either of Christ Himself or of someone by Him, yet he does not discuss these in the manner in which Origen does. If Lessing is going to use a lack of miracles as a motive to not "believe something which [his] reason refuses

---

[232] CC VII:32.

[233] Ibid, V:20.

[234] Ibid, II:58.

[235] Cf. "For the man was more than forty years old on whom this miracle [σημεῖον] of healing had been performed" (Acts 4:22 NASB). And, respectively: "And He could do no miracle[δύναμις] there except that He laid His hands on a few sick people and healed them" (Mark 6:5 NASB). The quote from Origen utilizes δύναμις.

to accept,"[236] and attempt to quote Origen to lend support to his case, it would help him to explore more fully what Origen actually has to say on the subject.

That Origen treats the resurrection as a "deep and hard" doctrine, then, creates difficulty for Lessing because it goes to show that Origen does not take the notion of "miracle" at face value. In fact, Origen does not seem to find miracles as being inherently persuasive. In as discussion of various claims to miracles, he says, "If the worship of Antinous were to be examined honestly and impartially, it would probably be found that it is owing to Egyptian magic and spells that he appears to do miracles in Antinoopolis even after his death... They set up in particular places daemons with the power to utter oracles or to heal... His virtues were invented by people who live by cheating."[237] In other words, miracles are not self-authenticating. Something more is required.

The element central to Origen's notion of the demonstration of power is, in fact, the conversion of sinners to a life of virtue. He says: "We would say that the soul of the bad man who is deluged with evil is deserted by God, and would maintain that the soul of the man who desires to live virtuously, or has even made some progress, or is even already living virtuously, is filled by or shares in a divine spirit."[238] Here it is shown that the presence of God is demonstrated in a desire to a life of virtue. He goes on to confidently "affirm that anyone who has received the coming of the Word of God into his own soul changes from bad to good, from licentiousness to self-control, and from superstition to piety."[239] Thus what is a divine action in the life of a person, the evidence of God's activity, is precisely

---

[236] Lessing, 86.
[237] CC III:36.
[238] Ibid, IV:5.
[239] Ibid, IV:5.

moral conversion. This certainly mitigates the attempt made by Lessing to commandeer Origen into supporting his argument that disbelief is justified simply because he does not see miraculous occurrences "with [his] own eyes."[240] If Lessing wants to use Origen as anything more than a misleading proof text, then he would need to change his argument to say that he sees no moral conversion before his eyes, and not simply miracle, but this might be harder for Lessing to argue.

To solidify the connection between Origen's understanding of "the demonstration of the spirit and of power" with moral conversion, it is noted that Origen says: "The *demonstration* in Jesus' apostles was given by God and *convinced* men *by spirit and power*. For this reason their word ran very quickly and sharply, or rather *God's Word* which was *working through them to change many of those who sin* by nature and by habit. Those whom a man could not change even by punishment, *the Word transformed, shaping and moulding them according to His will.*"[241] In other words, God's Word was demonstrating His spirit and power through the apostles by the change sinners, the transformation of sinners who were sinned "by nature and by habit." Origen makes no reference to supernatural action in contexts such as this other than moral reform.

Origen also says on this subject: "On account of this those who hear the word proclaimed with *power* are filled with power, *which they show forth by their sincerity and life* and by the fact that they fight to the death for truth."[242] It seems more or more clear that Origen's idea of the presence of God's power and spirit, the real miracle that is wrought is manifested not in instances of temporary miracles, but in a lasting change of

---

[240] Lessing, 84.
[241] CC III:69.
[242] Ibid, I:63.

character from the worse to the better. He even asks, "Why then is it outrageous if Jesus, wanting to show mankind the extent of his ability to heal souls, chose infamous and most wicked men, and led them on so far that they were an example of the purest moral character to those who were converted by them to the gospel of Christ?"[243] It was the miraculous moral transformation of wicked men's souls, therefore, that was the great example of Christ's power that Origen has in mind, the miracle of "bringing many to obey the word of God *by divine power.*"[244]

Lessing has also seemingly reduced miracle to the category of historical event, something which must be seen with the eyes, which is to say with the sense organs. Origen, however, communicates a different idea of this. He says concerning the vision of Ezekiel: "For I do not imagine that the *visible* heaven was opened, or its physical form divided, for Ezekiel to record such an experience."[245] In other words, certain supernatural events are correspondingly supersensible. It is thus not the eyes which see, but the mind which perceives. Origen, continuing, expands on the same notion and applies it to the New Testament: "Perhaps therefore the intelligent reader of the gospels ought to give a similar interpretation also in respect of the Saviour, even if this opinion may cause offence to the simple-minded, who in their extreme naiveté move the world and rend the vast, solid mass of the entire heaven."[246] Thus not merely restricted to Old Testament times, this type of supersensible supernatural event is simply part of the fabric of the Scriptural state of affairs. To critique miracle, then, as though it were always reducible to the sensible is a false assumption of Lessing, at least insofar as he uses Origen as an

---

[243] Ibid, I:64.
[244] Ibid, I:62.
[245] Ibid, I:48.
[246] Ibid.

authority to bolster his own arguments. Lessing, in trying to adopt Origen's notion of the demonstration of the spirit and of power not only finds therein something other than what he seemed to have in mind, but also a pivotal counterargument to one of his other central claims: that miracles, in order to be more than merely historically believable, must be sensibly seen. Origen himself, however, holds that seeing the miraculous with one's eyeballs is in some key cases not possible even in principle.

Origen asks in the context of a reference to the ability for a person to have true dreams forming images in their minds, either of "divine things" or "future events": "Why then is it strange to suppose that the force which forms an impression on the *mind* in a dream can also do so in the daytime for the benefit of the man on whom the impression is made, or for those who will hear about it from him?"[247] In other words, *contra* Lessing, seeing with one's physical eyes is not necessarily germane to the experience of true information about or coming from God. Not only this, according to Origen the communication of this vision to others is also *not* one of personal, empirical verification, but of believing what was reported vicariously to them by the one who experienced said supersensible vision. In other words, the experience can still be had "although these impressions are not experienced by our bodily eyes or made by any vibration in our ears, but are only in our *mind*."[248] Thus when Lessing states that "if he [Origen] had undoubted examples of this [i.e. miraculous phenomena], he had necessarily to acknowledge that proof of the spirit and of power if he did not wish to deny his own *senses*,"[249] it is demonstrated to the contrary, against Lessing's claim, that Origen's understanding of miracle is an issue of affirming empirical data coming from or to the senses. Origen's

---

[247] Ibid.
[248] Ibid.
[249] Lessing, 84.

understanding of the miraculous is neither coterminous with nor circumscribed by the senses. In fact, it is precisely *beyond* the senses and in the mind where Origen seems to most especially find the locus of miracle.

Origen calls this visionary experience "a certain generic divine sense."[250] More than merely the memory of an empirical experience, he further states that "there are many forms of this sense: a sight which can see things superior to corporeal beings, the cherubim or the seraphim being obvious instances, and a hearing which can receive impressions of sounds that have no objective existence in the air, and a taste which feeds on living bread that has come down from heaven and gives life to the world."[251] Origen even includes the sense of smell within this "divine sense," the supernatural and "superempirical" set of experiences related in Scripture. Of Jesus, Origen says in the same section that when He touched the leper it was both a physical touch, healing his common leprosy, and a divine touch, which healed a supernatural, primary leprosy. Furthermore, when John the Baptist bore witness to the descent of the Spirit in the form of a dove, Origen says, "It was to Jesus that the heavens were opened; and at that time no one but John is recorded to have seen the heavens opened."[252] Origen's idea of miracle is thus not primarily an issue of accepting or denying one's own senses, and so the argument of Lessing that relies on Origen's testimony of visible, empirical miracles is at best very flimsy.

Concerning the very identity of Christ as divine, which is especially denounced by Lessing when he asks, "must I therefore regard it as true that God has a Son who is of the same

---

[250] CC I:48.
[251] Ibid.
[252] Ibid.

essence as himself?"[253] Origen declares: "His divinity is testified by great numbers of churches, which consist of men converted from the flood of sins and who are dependent on the Creator and refer every decision to His pleasure."[254] Rather than temporary instances of miracles, the present proof of Christ's divinity, in Origen's time and arguably equally so in Lessing's, is actually the great miracle of the great numbers of churches within which people have been "converted from the flood of sins." The fact that Lessing has not carefully defined miracle is thus increasingly problematic for his argument, because what Origen holds to be the "visible" proof of Christ's very divinity is neither a mere issue of historical facticity, nor a necessarily sensible miracle, nor some obscure holy man's miracle working, but something that was arguably *not* outside of the realm of discoverability by Lessing: churches with people who are making progress in virtue.[255] Origen is unambiguous: "The goodness of Jesus towards men was not confined to the period of the incarnation only, but even to this day the *power* of Jesus brings about the *conversion* and *moral reformation* in those who believe in God through him. That this happens by his power is clearly *proved* by the fact that, as he himself said, and as experience proves... great is the harvest of people gathered in and collected into the threshing-floors of God, *which are churches.*"[256] Lessing's argument, then, at least insofar as it seeks

---

[253] Lessing, 86.

[254] CC I:47.

[255] In fact, John Wesley and George Whitefield, though not German, function fittingly to affirm Origen's notion of conversion-as-proof, for these men were noted for converting thousands and were contemporaries of Lessing. More generally, John Wesley was associated with the Pietism movement, which was also well-known in Germany along with the Moravians (such as Count Zinzendorf). Thus Lessing *could* have known of such conversion.

[256] CC I:44. See also CC I:67.

to use Origen, seems marred in that it does not fully take into account the presence of churches as an evidence of Christ's divinity, and so Lessing's very notion of what constitutes a miraculous proof is doubtful, and at the very least is taken inappropriately from Origen whose notion of proof was not demonstrably taken up by Lessing.

What is manifestly incredible about Lessing's argument is that, while denying historical miracle any role in claiming present persuasive power, he claims to not deny that the gospels are historically true: "I do not deny for a moment that prophecies were fulfilled in Christ; I do not deny for a moment that Christ performed miracles."[257] Origen, interestingly enough, gives a quite apt and prescient reply to Lessing's mode of argumentation here as it relates to Christ's divinity, especially given that Lessing says more than once that he does not deny the historicity of the gospel accounts. Origen, then, though refuting a past Celsus, as if also across future time, remarks: "For although he somehow accepts the incredible miracles which Jesus did, by which he persuaded the multitude to follow him as Christ, yet he wants to attack them as though they were done by magic and not by divine power."[258] For Origen it seems then as if the historical fact of miracles presents a transhistorical question: Either Christ is a mere magician or He is awesomely manifesting a power which is intrinsically transhistorical. Friend or foe, for Origen it thus seems that the manner in which one answers this question of miracles determines whether or not one "wants to attack them."

Though this issue will be taken up at greater length below, for the moment it is enough to note that Lessing has more likely quoted an enemy to his position when he has quoted

---

[257] Lessing, 87.
[258] CC I:38.

Irenaeus and Orthodox Apologetic Methodology

Origen, for Origen clearly sees that to accept the historicity of Christ's miracles is to thus be confronted not by a ditch to leap, but by an identity to confirm or deny. As Origen asks: "Who, therefore, that does not give merely a cursory study to the nature of the facts, would not be amazed at a man who overcame and was able to rise above all the factors that tended to discredit him, and in his reputation to surpass all the distinguished men that have ever lived?"[259] The fact that Lessing, as if nonplussed by the facts which he admits to accepting, can presume that a fact of history can be accepted and yet in its acceptance not have some intrinsic capacity attached to it which can transcend mere history. If *mere* history is such a thing that can exist would in itself be quite incredible.

It is in this context that Origen takes up another aspect of miracle which may be in Lessing's mind. Concerning fame, Origen says that some barbarians have become famous for "miraculous powers in incantations."[260] Thus we see a connection being made between miracle and incantation. One issue that comes up in relation to this statement is that the presence of incantatory miracles, as mere instances of power, is not restricted to either Christ or even to goodness. Concerning miraculous healings, in Origen's mind invocation is actually a science, and so for him this science does not produce a miracle that would necessarily prove Christ's divinity. Therefore, this type of miracle would not need to be experienced, at least in Lessing's sense, for the presence of this type of miracle does not intrinsically amount to proof, and could even be deceptive. As shown above, one oracle was seen by Origen as being energized by a daemon,[261] and so this type of miracle is not precisely what Origen would likely have had in mind when he spoke of the

---

[259] Ibid, I:30.
[260] Ibid, I:30.
[261] Ibid, III:36.

demonstration of the gospel, which as shown above was more fundamentally the conversion from sin.

The foregoing demonstrates that for Origen the notion of incantation/invocation is not restricted to Christians, and, after listing those who have this practice among themselves, such as the Persian magi, the Brahmans, the Samanaeans, "and so on according to each nation," says of the "nature of names" that it "is a consistent system, which has principles known to very few."[262] In other words, names were an Ancient esoteric science. What is more, "when the name of 'God' is linked with the names of these men a *miraculous* effect is produced among men."[263] In other words, according to Origen the miraculous effects produced by the invocation of special names is a miracle produced by and according to a science, and "if anyone is capable of understanding philosophically the mysterious significance of names,"[264] then they would see that there is nothing about this facet of the miraculous which would render it the fulcrum of faith, nor the absence of which that would function to discredit Christ's claim to divine Sonship. Since Origen understands that this type of "miracle" actually relates to a certain application of a particular skill and according to certain mysterious principles, then the absence of this "science" in Lessing's day would not be true evidence in favor of Lessing's argument, but could more properly be attributed either to a loss of this specific knowledge or perhaps to superstition. Since Lessing does not deny but affirms the historicity of the recorded miracles, then he would seem to be forced into the former category rather than the latter, meaning that for Lessing this

---

[262] Ibid, I:24.
[263] Ibid, I:25.
[264] Ibid.

Irenaeus and Orthodox Apologetic Methodology

type of miracle ought not be requisite for believing Christ's divinity, nor the absence of it in his own time an obstacle.[265]

Moreover, concerning the doubt-worthiness of the miracle seemingly required by Lessing for faith, Origen states: "If the worship of Antinous were to be examined honestly and impartially, it would probably be found that it is owing to Egyptian magic and spells that he appears to do miracles in Antinoopolis *even after his death*... They set up in particular places daemons with the power to utter oracles or to heal."[266] In short, *contra* Lessing's use of Origen, miracles can be the result of supernatural evil.[267] This seems to underscore why moral reformation plays such an important role in Origen's understanding as the truer miracle proving Christ's divinity. Since miracles can be supernatural and yet false, perhaps the result of sorcery,[268] it is therefore not to the empirical that one must turn, but to the moral. As Origen says: "How much superior to this was it for God to make use of a voice *which effected conviction* in those who heard in some indescribable way, because it was proclaimed with *power*."[269] God's power, therefore, at least according to Origen, is that which effects conviction in those who, in some indescribable way, hear it.

---

[265] Concerning the doubt-worthiness of the miracle seemingly required by Lessing for faith, see CC III:36: "If the worship of Antinous were to be examined honestly and impartially, it would probably be found that it is owing to Egyptian magic and spells that he appears to do miracles in Antinoopolis even after his death... They set up in particular places daemons with the power to utter oracles or to heal." This seems to underscore why moral reformation plays such an important role in Origen's understanding of the true miracle of Christ's divinity.

[266] CC III:36.

[267] Cf. CC IV:33-34 and V:45-46

[268] CC I:68.

[269] Ibid, I:70.

The foregoing discussion ought to be sufficient proof that Origen's own position is better described as alien and hostile to Lessing's. Origen states, perhaps disdaining Lessing's empirical, "sensational" notion of miracles, again as if responding across the centuries, that "Jesus is always being falsely accused, and there is never a time when he is not being accused so long as there is evil among men. He is still silent in face of this and does not answer with his voice; but he makes his defence in the *lives* of his genuine disciples, for their lives cry out the real facts and defeat all false charges, refuting and overthrowing the slanders and accusations."[270] In other words, Origen does not rest the truth of the Christian faith on contemporary magical miracles or on what can be perceived merely by an amazement of the senses, "for the divine voice is such that it is heard only by those whom the speaker wishes to hear it… the utterance of God is certainly not vibrated air… because it is heard by a superior sense, more divine than physical hearing."[271] Miracle of that sort is thus not reducible to proof-on-demand; Christ even associates this mentality with evil.[272] The real miracle, then, the real proof, is the striving after of virtue as found in His genuine disciples.[273] It would seem that according to Origen, then, Lessing's proclaimed need for a present empirical miracle is unfounded and misguided.

A further problem here is that if Lessing accepts the historicity of Christ's miracles, as he claims to do, but then refuses their significance based on a sophistry as to the nature of "contingent truths of history," he thereby places Christ in the

---

[270] Ibid, Praef. 2.

[271] Ibid, II:72. For Origen's idea that even supernatural healings are not fully conclusive or persuasive: CC III:24-5.

[272] Luke 11:29. Cf. Mark 8:12.

[273] "We know love by this, that He laid down His life for us; and we ought to lay down our lives for the brethren" (1 John 3:16).

awkward position of either being who and what He said He was, and therefore is, or Christ is merely a teacher of self-evident and "necessary truths of reason" but is otherwise questionable as to the nature of His other statements. Is Christ lying? Then how could Lessing claim to accept the truth of the history? Is Christ telling the truth? Since Christ's own claims within the gospels would by definition transcend the merely historical, and if Lessing accepts, as he says he does, that Christ really did and said these things, and so is telling the truth, having performed miracles which Lessing also accepts, then on what ground does Lessing trivialize the self-attesting unity of Christ's claims to divinity relative to His actions? Yet Origen could be seen to critique Lessing's hermeneutic on another level: "The truth of the events recorded to have happened to Jesus cannot be fully seen in the mere text and historical narrative; for each event to those who read the Bible more intelligently is clearly a symbol of something as well."[274] In other words, the events recorded in the gospels are, according to Origen, precisely intended to extend beyond reflection of a merely historical nature, which is to say that the historical narrative *does* motivate towards Christ's "other teachings," to that "quite different class of truths."[275]

Origen, the very author Lessing uses to dig his ditch, to use Lessing's own phrase, "is not very helpful if one omits to tell one's readers what Origen says... afterwards."[276] By reading Origen selectively, Lessing has erected a false dilemma between truths of history and truths of reason. One might even ask Lessing whether truths of reason which were not demonstrable

---

[274] CC II:69.
[275] Lessing, 87.
[276] Ibid, 85.

from history were in fact "necessary."[277] Origen, however, seeing yet no conflict with history as a source of veridical persuasion, states: "I think that the clear and certain proof is the argument from the behavior of the disciples, who devoted themselves to a teaching which involved risking their lives."[278] History can thus alone provide "clear and certain proof."

Moreover, demonstrating the unity of Origen's thought on the subject, and concerning the manner in which Origen sees this extending into his own day, one might ask with Origen: "the *doctrines*... have been filled with power as though they were spells, and when we see that the *words* turn multitudes all at once from being licentious to living the most tranquil life, and from being unrighteous to nobility of character, and from being cowards or effeminate to such bravery that they even despise death for the sake of the piety which they believe to be right, are we not justified in admiring the power in the message?"[279] Thus, when Lessing attempts to state that Origen's proof is "primarily and specifically through the miracles which were still happening then,"[280] it seems that Lessing has deeply misunderstood Origen's understanding of the nature of history and of miracle, and so his complaint, rooted in Origen, that the "proof of the proof has now completely disappeared"[281] is either really a lament that virtue and moral rectitude have "completely disappeared" from the Church, or is simply the result of a misunderstanding and misrepresentation of Origen's own views.

---

[277] Especially since any and all empirical verification is immediately reduced to a matter of history.
[278] CC II:56.
[279] Ibid, III:68. Cf. Romans 1:16.
[280] Lessing, 85.
[281] Ibid.

Irenaeus and Orthodox Apologetic Methodology

Digging into Lessing's Ditch

Now that it has been shown that Lessing has not accurately portrayed or utilized the thought of Origen, I would like to examine some further key statements by Lessing in light of the above. It is clear that he is making ado about the limitations of historical knowledge, and baulking at the idea of relying on the testimony of others. As he says, "If no historical truth can be demonstrated, then nothing can be demonstrated by means of historical truth. That is, contingent truths of history can never become the proof of necessary truths of reason."[282] In other words, for Lessing there is nothing intrinsic to historical testimony compelling him to believe. As he says, "Miracles which I see with my own eyes, and have an opportunity to assess, are one thing; miracles of which I know only from history that others claim to have seen and assessed them are another."[283] Mere reports of miracles and mere reports of fulfillment of prophecies are not enough to inspire faith, though if he had seen them, he claims of himself: "I would willingly have subordinated my understanding to his [Christ's] and believed him in all matters in which equally indubitable experiences did not contradict him."[284] He says he would have believed Christ had he seen him, and that he would also believe if he witnessed "genuine miracles" in his own day.[285]

This position, however, is strained by other statements of his. For example, he says, "I do not deny for a moment that prophecies were fulfilled in Christ; I do not deny for a moment that Christ performed miracles."[286] He makes other statements

---

[282] Ibid.
[283] Ibid, 84.
[284] Ibid.
[285] Ibid.
[286] Ibid, 86.

Irenaeus and Orthodox Apologetic Methodology

similar to this, that he does not "deny" that the historical reports are "as reliable as historical truths can ever be."[287] Yet this is precisely the issue, for much of Lessing's argument hinges on this mitigation, this reduction of the status of trust in historical reports and the categorical diminution of their persuasive value. He wants to say he believes the reports, that he does not deny them, yet at the same time this belief and this non-denial operate in a denuded sphere which in his mind does not in any way translate into a motive to religious belief. Despite not denying these "undisputed and indisputable... reports," he yet denies "that they can and should bind me to the least faith in the other teachings of Christ."[288] Suffice it to say that he claims, as if from one side of his mouth, that he does not deny them, that they are indisputable, yet on the other side that they are not grounds for accepting the "other teachings" of Christ.

  A vital question, then, and one which is not addressed by Lessing, is how one can accept miracle *as miracle* and yet deny it meaning beyond the merely empirical. How can a miracle be a miracle and yet not carry the *significance* implied by the miracle? Furthermore, on what grounds does he deny history the capacity to transmit binding truths, categorically partitioning it off as he does from the so-called necessary truths of reason, which is to say, how does history become emptied of metaphysical content and significance?

  Since the term miracle, rooted Biblically in the concept of sign, such as Christ's raising Lazarus from the dead, as Lessing refers to, denotes something more than a contentless supernatural event, as Lessing openly claims to accept, he places the reader in a bind. The term miracle, which is to say sign

---

[287] Ibid, 85.
[288] Ibid, 86.

(σημεῖον), is understood as something which points beyond itself. Thus, to accept "the miracle" is not to accept so much the mere material historical fact, but the very thing to which it points to as a sign. The miracles of Christ were pointers not to themselves, but to the identity of the Person performing or enabling them. A defining moment of this aspect of Biblical miracle is found in Luke: "When the men came to Him, they said, 'John the Baptist has sent us to You, to ask, 'Are You the Expected One, or do we look for someone else?'"[289] In other words, when the identity of Jesus is being inquired into, the answer to be given is key: "And He answered and said to them, 'Go and report to John what you have seen and heard: the BLIND RECEIVE SIGHT, the lame walk, the lepers are cleansed, and the deaf hear, the dead are raised up, the POOR HAVE THE GOSPEL PREACHED TO THEM.'"[290] In other words, the miracles served precisely as identity markers, and as such to identify Christ as the Expected One, and so to accept the miracles is nothing less than to accept the Person to which they point.

This is a real problem for Lessing's argument. Since he emphatically affirms that he accepts the miracles as indisputable historical facts, and yet denies the essential ingredient of the miracle, which is the identity of the Person to which said miracle points, then Lessing has asserted a confusion and a contradiction, if not a self-refutation. It would be akin to accepting that water flows downhill while denying that this binds him to believe that it is liquid, or that it is liquid and yet deny that it binds him to believe it is wet. Water, however, flows because it is liquid, and liquid water and wetness are bound together by nature, if not by definition, and likewise the

---

[289] Luke 7:20
[290] Ibid, 7:22.

miracles of Christ point precisely to the divine power of the Person energizing them, the action being inextricably bound to the identity of the Person performing the action. Put even more simply, it would be like accepting that a stop sign *says* stop, but denying that it *means* stop.

At its most basic, miracle is "miracle" precisely because in its very factness it points to a noncontingent, transhistorical origin. Thus to attempt to state that one accepts the miracle without accepting what miracle means does not work. If it is a miracle, then it is a *miracle*; if it is fulfilled prophecy, then it is fulfilled *prophecy*; if it *is* these things, then the superempirical and transhistorical dimension likewise *is* intrinsic to the very things Lessing does "willingly accept."[291] If he really does accept these, then by virtue of their very definition they could not be imprisoned within a categorical dungeon of historical contingency, outlawed from the kingdom of necessary truths of reason.

Lessing's ditch therefore, in principle, cannot be solved from within the confines of his setting up of the problem, because the set-up is itself a confusion, and yet this set-up is entirely what sustains the ditch. Moreover, it is the very leaping which creates it. As long as one accepts Lessing's set-up, then one has already implicitly conceded to the ditch's insolubility. This is so because of the manner in which Lessing has denuded history of metaphysical significance. Lessing's distortion of miracle is emblematic of this, for if accepted it leads one to accept the term emptied of its essential content, meanwhile suggesting that one leap to the meaning which has already in principle been denied. Saying that a miracle or prophecy of Christ does not essentially and transhistorically point to the presence of the divine in the Person who performed or

---

[291] Lessing, 87.

proclaimed it, yet somehow accept that "it" happened (which is what keeps the person leaping), and then suggest that one magically leap to this (intrinsically denied) meaning while at the same time still maintaining that the miracle does not essentially mean what it means, is simply to set up a revolving self-contradiction. In the very act of leaping to the significance one must deny the significance, because the ground from which one leaps is the denial of the significance of the thing one is leaping to. In other words, the very leaping creates the ditch; and the harder one tries to leap, the further recedes the sought after ledge. Thus Lessing can never leap his ditch, nor can anyone else, because, in leaping, one's argument has already internalized unleapability. No one can leap to a meaning one rejects in principle.

As Lessing says, "the fact that these historians [the gospel writers] were inspired is unfortunately *only* historically certain. This, this is the broad and ugly ditch which I cannot get across."[292] Well, since history has been denied any transempirical or metaphysical significance, it should be obvious why he cannot get across, for one cannot *by means of* an anti-metaphysic leap to a positive metaphysic. This then exposes one of Lessing's deepest problems, for the foregoing statement of Lessing is not so much a ditch separating two mere positions, or even conclusions, but is actually the necessary effect of an incompatibility between two contrary metaphysical "worldviews."

The first metaphysic presupposes the merely empirical nature of history. In this view, history is not and cannot ever be a source of reliable truth, such that even if one were to accept some so-called fact of material history, this acceptance can only and even must only ever be provisional. The other, jarringly

---

[292] Ibid.

juxtaposed metaphysic is the one in which rational theological reflection can be and necessarily is bound up with historical fact. In this view, God, as the creator and sustainer of reality, the architect, so to speak, of history, and the inspirer of Scriptural witness, Himself functions as the integral source of meaning, relevance, and reliability to factual history generally, and to sacred history specifically, where history is not an obstacle to belief but is instead an inescapable component of it. Thus, whichever metaphysic one leaps from, the other can never be lept to, for each intrinsically denies the other's motivating hypothesis.

This confusion is only compounded by Lessing when he says he accepts the historicity of events such as Christ's resurrection. If he had denied it, then it would be clearly a matter of choosing metaphysical "sides." But since he claims to accept it, it generates a wrinkle in the mind of the reader because it seems there is this riddle concerned with how to get from historical fact to theological truth. To accept the resurrection *as resurrection*, however, is precisely to accept the position contrary to the one set up by Lessing. Thus a "believer" who accepts the premises of the ditch is caught in a truly distressing conundrum, for he wants to somehow "superaccept" the position he already he accepts, placing his prior acceptance in question; for to accept the ditch is to accept a denial of the significance of the very thing he is seeking to affirm, in this case the resurrection. The distress enters because it seems as though the believer can never quite arrive at true belief in the significance of the historical resurrection because its meaning as a historical event has been denied any metaphysical significance *in principle*.[293] On the other hand, the "unbeliever" who accepts

---

[293] One method of dealing with this problem could be derived from the teaching of creation *ex nihilo*. According to this, since creation is not self-existing, but takes its origin, sustenance, meaning, and end in God, it would

the premises of the ditch is in some sense insulated from belief and galvanized in unbelief because there is already present the denial of the meaning of the resurrection such that to either accept or deny its historicity at this point ends up a trivial affair. The result is that the ditch in some sense functions to lend itself to unbelief.

It might be asked, then, is Lessing's ditch a true or a false dilemma? The argument from the above discussion points to the conclusion that Lessing's ditch is a false dilemma born of erecting self-contradictory categories. It could be likened to the "Liar Paradox," where one encounters a phrase such as: "This sentence is a lie." If the Liar Paradox is accepted, the more one shows the truth of the phrase, the more one asserts that it is a lie, and therefore false; and the more one asserts that it is false, the more one shows that it is true, and therefore a lie. Ironically, one might say that it is "truly false," and likewise Lessing's ditch is truly false. The ditch itself, then, seems to be the symbol of two alien worldviews, one in which history is incorporated into an integrated field of rational inquiry and where trustworthy history can function holistically to point beyond the merely historical, and another worldview in which history is denied meaningful access to what ends up being a fragmented field of inquiry, where history is relativised such that it *cannot* meaningfully point beyond itself.

---

thus not be *possible* to separate history from theology. As one historian stated: "History can and must be interpreted only in terms of that ultimate meaning which God conferred upon it in the act of creation. Thus, the subsequent history of man on earth derives its meaning from this original act of creation" (Singer, Gregg C.; "The Problem of Historical Interpretation"; in *Foundations of Christian Scholarship*; Vallecito: Ross House Books, 1976; 64). According to Singer: "History is neither self-originating nor self-sustaining. Neither can time exist in and of itself" (ibid). Thus, in principle, history is intrinsically bound up with theology, and theology cannot be a separate "class" of truths.

The statement perhaps most emblematic of these two alien worldviews is when Lessing states that he lives "in the eighteenth century in which miracles no longer happen."[294] In other words, Lessing is clearly coming at the question with a prior metaphysical commitment, one in which miracles do not happen. Relative to his ditch, however, his own question can be rephrased and asked: If nothing can be rightly demonstrated by means of factual history, then can anything be rightly denied that is coextensive with said historical claims? In other words, if Lessing claims to accept the history of the gospels, yet removes history from the category of necessary proof, then history is silenced as a witness *either pro or con*. History simply does not speak to the issue, if history could even be said to speak to anything at all at this point. Thus, the empirical verification of even a contemporary "miracle" could only ever be a matter of history, for once experienced and reported it is thereby reduced to the category of contingent history; according to Lessing, then, even an eighteenth century miracle would also cease to be a valid warrant for belief.

Since personal experience of a miracle, or anything else for that matter, is by definition not a truth that is transferable beyond the contingent report of a personal experience by some individual, written or spoken, the question for Lessing becomes how an experienced miracle ever *could* become the ground for a "necessary truth of reason." Even if Lessing's most trusted friend had experienced a miracle, it could not meet Lessing's criteria for the simple reason that Lessing had not himself experienced it. In short, to be necessary it must be personally experienced. To follow this reasoning, even if every person on the planet had experienced a miracle, except for Lessing, Lessing would still be obligated by his own criteria to refuse admittance of these

---

[294] Lessing, 84.

contingent claims.[295] But if he did experience a miracle, and yet no one else did, according to Lessing his personal experience of this miracle would become a necessary truth, at least of *his* reasoning, for certainly his experience of a miracle would be a necessary truth of reason lest "he deny his own senses."[296] But if this personal experience is admitted, if an experience of miracle *can* function in the context of a *necessary* truth of reason, then so is everyone else's experiences of miracle.[297] For surely a truth of reason cannot be necessary for some and not for others; either it is necessary or it is not necessary.

    This, then, seriously blurs the line between the contingent truths of history and the necessary truths of reason. At this point, if the necessary truth of reason is now arbitrated merely on the basis of the presence or absence of a *de facto* non-universal and contingent personal experience, then in what sense can it be a *necessary* truth of reason? Is reason not universal? Can a truth be necessary for some but not for others? Since in principle no subjective experience is transferable, then either no experience can be admitted into the "class" of necessary truths of reason, not even experiences of the miraculous, or experience can be admitted into the "class" of necessary truths of reason. Yet if contingency is not a true obstacle, if experience of a miracle *can* be admitted into the class of necessary truths of reason, then on what basis can Lessing deny that others' experience of miracle can be bindingly admitted into his own reasoning if it is merely on the basis that they are contingent? Simply because they are not his own personal experiences? But this means that it is not a necessary truth of reason that is demanded, but a contingent one, and so

---

[295] This would be like a blind person denying that colors are real.

[296] Lessing, 84. This could then justify almost any delusional claim.

[297] In other words, if it was a necessary truth of reason for everyone on the planet except Lessing, it would still not be a necessary truth for Lessing!

on unto some type of philosophical individualism, for he has admitted that only a personal and therefore contingent experience of a miracle would necessitate belief in its significance.

Lessing has thus turned himself, and so the individual, into the absolute arbiter of necessary truth claims. Since to experience a miracle is to have the necessary truth of reason regarding the significance of said miracle, a necessary truth which in principle cannot be communicated to others as a necessary truth, where only experienced truth is necessary truth, then the truth itself is arbitrarily determined by the individual who possesses said contingent historical truth. Lessing's version of necessary truth is therefore not universally necessary, and furthermore is not binding unless possessed of a particular, contingent, and non-universal experience. One might ask: are the necessary truths of reason then just the sum of contingent truths? In short, his necessary truth is not necessary truth at all, but "personal" truth. Lessing's argument, then, if taken to its further consequence, is absurd, for if truth is merely personal then if it can ascend even beyond opinion it yet cannot ascend to but relative necessity, which is a contradiction in terms.

On one hand Lessing states that belief is not necessitated by contingent historical truth but by necessary truths of reason, whereas on the other hand the necessary truths of reason are entirely determined by whether or not one has experienced a contingent historical truth. Thus, in outwardly mitigating, if not denying, the role of contingent truth, he drives the argument onto purely rational grounds, in which case he also denies the ground of the claim that personal experience can ascend to the class of necessary truth. If experience, however, can ascend to the class of necessary truth, then either he accepts as persuasive others' experience as well as his own, or he falls into the absurd by saying that only *his* personal experience warrants being a necessary truth of reason. But if contingent truth is only necessary for the experiencer, and *in very principle* unnecessary for everyone else, then reason is no longer necessary but is itself contingent. Thus Lessing's whole enterprise falls apart.

Given, then, Lessing's confused view of contingent historical truth, for him to settle on whether or not Christ is the Son of God, he would have to avoid the question of history altogether, which would actually make it impossible to speak to the question of Christ at all. The question is thus not whether he is compelled to believe on this or that ground, but on whether or not what is said of Christ is true. In treating the subject as he has, in a fascinating way Lessing has actually changed the focus from whether or not the gospel is true to whether or not it needs to be believed. According to Lessing, since the gospel is historical, it therefore in principle does not warrant belief since it is not constituted of a truly valid means of necessary knowledge, and so the effect of Lessing's ditch is to make the history *unbelievable* by sidestepping the issue of whether or not it is *true* - even *if* it were absolutely true. Of course, if it were absolutely true, it would be binding, but the force of Lessing's argument is to make even what could be absolutely and bindingly true into something fundamentally unbelievable.

Conclusion

Though much more could be said, especially concerning the relationship between personal experience and the knowledge of truth, and other important issues touched upon, such as what motivates the radical mistrust of vicarious testimony, what has been discussed thus far has sought to show that Lessing's ditch is a pseudo-problem. Despite the fact that it poses as a genuine conundrum, the real problem is found in the manner in which it is set up. Therefore, the solution is found in unraveling the confusion out of which it is woven. Not only does Lessing misrepresent Origen's thought concerning what the "proof of the spirit and of power" fundamentally is, but moreover creates an untenable composition of presuppositions concerning the nature and relationship of sensory experience, history, truth, and reason. In short, there is no ditch. Solving the problem at the level of the problem is like trying to solve the Liar's Paradox, which is to say, Lessing's ditch is not solved on the level at which it is presented. The ditch is created in the very leaping which Lessing's image sets the well-meaning theologian to jumping. One cannot, however, jump what is unreal.

BIBLIOGRAPHY

Andreyev, I. M. *Orthodox Apologetic Theology*. Platina, CA: St. Herman of Alaska Brotherhood, 1995.

Aristotle. *The Basics Works of Aristotle*. ed. McKeon, Richard. New York, NY: The Modern Library, 2001.

____. *The Organon*. ed. Jones, Roger Bishop. Self-published from MIT classics archive, 2013.

Athanasius. *Against the Heathen*. tr. Robertson, Archibald. Nicene and Post-Nicene Fathers, Second Series, vol. 4. ed. Schaff, Philip and Wace, Henry. Buffalo, NY: Christian Literature Publishing Co., 1892.

____. *Discourses Against the Arians*. tr. Newman, John Henry and Robertson, Archibald. Nicene and Post-Nicene Fathers, Second Series, vol. 4. ed. Schaff, Philip and Wace, Henry. Buffalo, NY: Christian Literature Publishing Co., 1892.

____. *Works on the Spirit: Athanasius the Great and Didymus the Blind*. tr. DelCogliano, Mark; Radde-Gallwitz, Andrew; and Ayres, Lewis. Yonkers, NY: St Vladimir's Press, 2011.

Bahnsen, Greg. *Always Ready: Directions for Defending the Faith*. Nacogdoches: Covenant Media Press, 1996.

____. *Presuppositional Apologetics: Stated and Defended*. Ed. McDurmon, Joel. Powder Springs: The American Vision. Nacogdoches: Covenant Media Press, 2011.

____. *Van Til's Apologetic: Readings and Analysis*. Phillipsburg: Presbyterian and Reformed Publishing, 1998.

Bavinck, Herman. *The Philosophy of Revelation*. Grand Rapids, MI: Baker Book House, 1979.

Behr, John. *Irenaeus of Lyons: Identifying Christianity*. Oxford: Oxford University Press, 2013.

____. *The Mystery of Christ: Life in Death*. Crestwood, NY: St. Vladimir's Seminary Press, 2006.

____. *The Nicene Faith: The Formation of Christian Theology: Vol 2; Part 1*. Crestwood, NY: St Vladimir's Seminary Press, 2004.

____. *The Nicene Faith: The Formation of Christian Theology: Vol 2; Part 2*. Crestwood, NY: St Vladimir's Seminary Press, 2004.

____. *The Way to Nicaea: The Formation of Christian Theology: Vol 1*. Crestwood, NY: St Vladimir's Seminary Press, 2001.

Blowers, Paul. "The *Regula Fidei* and the Narrative Character of Early Christian Faith." *Pro Ecclesia* 6, no. 2 (1997): 199-228.

Bochenski, J.M. *The Methods of Contemporary Thought*. New York, NY: Harper and Row, 1968.

Briggman, Anthony. *Irenaeus of Lyons and the Theology of the Holy Spirit*. Oxford: Oxford University Press, 2012.

Buchler, Justus. *The Concept of Method*. New York: Columbia University Press, 1961.

Christian Apologetics Past and Present: A Primary Source Reader (Volume 2, From 1500). eds. Edgar, William and Oliphint, K. Scott. Wheaton: Crossway, 2011.

Clark, Gordon. *A Christian View of Men and Things: An Introduction to Philosophy*. Grand Rapids, MI: Baker Book House, 1952.

____. *In Defense of Theology*. Milford, MI: Mott Media, 1984.

____. *An Introduction to Christian Philosophy*. Unicoi, TN: Trinity Foundation, 1993.

____. *Karl Barth's Theological Method*. Unicoi, TN: Trinity Foundation, 1963.

____. *Religion, Reason, and Revelation*. Unicoi, TN: Trinity Foundation, 1995.

____. *Thales to Dewey*. Jefferson, MD: The Trinity Foundation, 1989.

____. *Three Types of Religious Philosophy*. Unicoi, TN: Trinity Foundation, 1989.

Clark, Kelly James. *Return to Reason*. Grand Rapids: Eerdmans, 1990.

Clouser, Roy. *The Myth of Religious Neutrality: An Essay on the Hidden Role of Religious Belief in Theories*. Notre Dame: Notre Dame Press, 1991.

Craig, William Lane. *Advice to Christian Apologists*. <http://www.bethinking.org/apologetics/advice-to-christian-apologists>, May 9, 2015.

____. *On Guard: Defending Your Faith with Reason and Precision*. Colorado Springs, CO: David Cook, 2010.

____. *Reasonable Faith: Christian Truth and Apologetics*. 3rd ed. Wheaton, IL: Crossway, 2008.

Damick, Andrew Steven. *Orthodoxy and Heterodoxy: Exploring Belief Systems Through
the Lens of the Ancient Christian Faith*. Chesterton, IN: Conciliar Press, 2011.

Dulles, Avery Cardinal. *A History of Apologetics*. San Francisco, CA: Ignatius Press, 2005.

Faith and Rationality: Reason and Belief in God. eds. Plantinga, Alvin and Wolterstorff, Nicholas. Notre Dame: Notre Dame Press, 1983.

Five Views on Apologetics. ed. Cowan, Steven B. Grand Rapids, MI: Zondervan, 2000.

Foundations of Christian Scholarship: Essays in the Van Til Perspective. ed. North, Gary. Vallecito: Ross House Books, 1976.

Frame, John. *Apologetics to the Glory of God: An Introduction*. Phillipsburg: Presbyterian and Reformed Publishing, 1994.

____. *Cornelius Van Til: An Analysis of His Thought*. Phillipsburg: Presbyterian and Reformed Publishing, 1995.

____. *The Doctrine of God*. Phillipsburg: Presbyterian and Reformed Publishing, 2002.

____. *The Doctrine of the Knowledge of God*. Phillipsburg: Presbyterian and Reformed Publishing, 1987.

Geisler, Norman. *Christian Apologetics*. Grand Rapids: Baker Book House, 1976.

Grant, Robert M. *Irenaeus of Lyons*. New York, NY: Routledge, 1997.

Gregory of Nyssa. *Contra Eunomius*. tr. Moore, W.; Wilson, H.A.; and Ogle, H.C. Nicene and Post-Nicene Fathers, Second Series. vol 5. ed. Schaff, Philip and Wace, Henry. Christian Literature Publishing Company, 1892.

Habermas, Gary. *The Historical Jesus: Ancient Evidence for the Life of Christ*. Joplin, MO: College Press Publishing, 1996.

Habermas, Gary and Licona, Michael. *The Case for the Resurrection of Jesus*. Grand Rapids, MI: Kregel Publications, 2004.

Hart, David Bentley. *Atheist Delusions: The Christian Revolution and its Fashionable Enemies*. New Haven, CT: Yale University Press, 2009.

Hefner, Philip. "Theological Methodology and St. Irenaeus." The Journal of Religion, Vol. 44, No. 4 (Oct., 1964), pp. 294-309.

Irenaeus of Lyons. *Adversus Haereses*. Tr. Roberts, Alexander and Rambaut, William. *Ante-Nicene Fathers*, Vol. 1. ed. Roberts, Alexander; Donaldson, James; and Coxe, A. Cleveland. Buffalo, NY: Christian Literature Publishing Co., 1885.

____. *Libros Quinque Adversus Haereses*, 2 vols. ed. Harvey, W. Cantabrigiae: Typis academicis, 1857.

____. *On the Apostolic Preaching*. tr. John Behr. Popular Patristic Series, Number 17. Crestwood, NY: St Vladimir's Seminary Press, 1997.

Irenaeus: Life, Scripture, Legacy. eds. Parvis, Sara and Foster, Paul. Minneapolis, MN: Fortress Press, 2012.

John of Damascus. *Saint John of Damascus: Writings*. tr. Frederic H. Chase, Jr. The Fathers of the Church: vol. 37. Washington D.C.: The Catholic University of America Press, 1958.

____. *Three Treatises on the Divine Images*. tr. Louth, Andrew. Crestwood, NY: St Vladimir's Seminary Press, 2003.

Kreeft, Peter. *Fundamentals of the Faith: Essays in Christian Apologetics*. San Francisco: Ignatius Press, 1988.

____. *Socratic Logic: A Logic Text Using Socratic Method, Platonic Questions, and Aristotelian Principles*. ed. 3.1. South Bend, IN: St. Augustine's Press, 2010.

Kreeft, Peter and Tacelli, Ronald. *Handbook of Christian Apologetics*. Downers Grove: Intervarsity Press. 1994.

Lewis, Gordon R. *Testing Christianity's Truth Claims: Approaches to Christian Apologetics*. Chicago, IL: Moody Press, 1976.

Mathison, Keith. *The Shape of Sola Scriptura*. Moscow, ID: Canon Press, 2001.

McDowell, Josh. *Evidence That Demands a Verdict: Historical Evidences for the Christian Faith*. vol 1. rev. San Bernardino: CA, Here's Life Publishers, 1979.

Minns, Denis. *Irenaeus: An Introduction*. New York, NY: T&T Clark International, 2010.

Montgomery, John Warwick. *Faith Founded on Fact: Essays in Evidential Apologetics*. Newburgh, IN: Trinity Press, 1978.

Moreland, J.P. and Craig, William Lane. *Philosophical Foundations for a Christian Worldview*. Downers Grove, IL: InterVarsity Press, 2003.

Morris, Thomas. *The Logic of God Incarnate*. Eugene, OR: Wipf and Stock Publishers, 2001.

Oliphint, K. Scott. *Revelation and Reason: New Essays in Reformed Apologetics*. Phillipsburg: Presbyterian and Reformed Publishing, 2007.

Osborn, Eric. *Irenaeus of Lyons*. Cambridge: Cambridge University Press, 2001.

Payton, James R. *Irenaeus on the Christian Faith: A Condensation of Against Heresies*. Eugene, OR: Wipf & Stock Pub, 2011.

Plantinga, Alvin. *God and Other Minds: A Study of the Rational Justification of Belief in God*. Ithaca, NY: Cornell University Press, 1990.

____. *The Nature of Necessity*. Oxford: Oxford University Press, 1979.

____. *Warranted Christian Belief*. Oxford: Oxford University Press, 2000.

Quasten, Johannes. *Patrology: Vol. 1, The Beginnings of Patristic Literature*. Westminster, MD: The Newman Press, 1962.

Rose, Seraphim. *Nihilism: The Root of the Revolution of the Modern Age*. Platina, CA: St Herman Press, 2001.

Schmemann, Alexander. *For the Life of the World: Sacraments and Orthodoxy*. Crestwood, NY: St Vladimir's Seminary Press, 2004.

Schooping, Joshua. "John of Damascus and Christian Discourse: The *Dialectica* Viewed as a Neopatristic Metastructure in Light of Florovsky, Gadamer, and Ricoeur." *International Journal of Orthodox Theology* 7:3 (2016).

Swinburne, Richard. *The Coherence of Theism*. rev. Oxford: Oxford University Press, 1993.

____. *The Existence of God*. rev. Oxford: Oxford University Press, 1991.

____. *Faith and Reason*. 2nd ed. Oxford: Oxford University Press, 2005.

Van Til, Cornelius. *Christian Apologetics*. Second Edition. ed. Edgar, William. Phillipsburg: Presbyterian and Reformed Publishing, 2003.

____. *A Christian Theory of Knowledge*. Phillipsburg: Presbyterian and Reformed Publishing, 1969.

____. *Christianity and Barthianism*. Phillipsburg: Presbyterian and Reformed Publishing, 1962.

____. *The Defense of the Faith*. Fourth Edition. Ed. Oliphint, K. Scott. Phillipsburg: Presbyterian and Reformed Publishing, 2008.

____. *In Defense of the Faith: Vol II: A Survey of Christian Epistemology*. Second Edition. Phillipsburg: Presbyterian and Reformed Publishing, 1932.

____. *An Introduction to Systematic Theology*. Second Edition. ed. Edgar, William. Phillipsburg: Presbyterian and Reformed Publishing, 1974.

Wuellner, Bernard, S.J. *Dictionary of Scholastic Philosophy*. Fitzwilliam, NH: Loreto Publications, 2012.

Printed in Great Britain
by Amazon